The Complete Guide To
Auto Body Repair

The Complete Guide To
Auto Body Repair

Dennis W. Parks

DEDICATION

To Roger Ward, the best body man I have ever known. Doane Spencer built a
1932 Ford roadster that made hot rodders want to build roadsters, but Roger built
a 1951 Chevrolet station wagon that made hot rodders want to build station wagons.
Now, that is making a statement . . .

First published in 2008 by Motorbooks, an imprint of MBI Publishing Company, 400 First Avenue North, Suite 300, Minneapolis, MN 55401 USA.

Motorbooks titles are also available at discounts in bulk quantity for industrial or sales-promotional use. For details write to Special Sales Manager at MBI Publishing Company, 400 First Avenue North, Suite 300, Minneapolis, MN 55401 USA.

To find out more about our books, join us online at www.motorbooks.com.

ISBN-13: 978-0-7603-3278-8

Editor: James Manning Michels
Designer: Chris Fayers

Printed in Singapore

On the cover, main: Disassembly and reassembly are integral to auto body repair.

Inset: Stud welders are used to temporarily weld small metal rods to sheet metal so you have something to grab onto when pulling out dents.

On the title page: The salmon (pink) color on this firewall and cowl is weld-through primer. The primer provides short-term protection for the metal surface but does not have to be ground away prior to doing any welding.

On the back cover: The curved end of this hammer allows you to strike a surface even in tight situations.

About the author
Dennis Parks is a professional technical writer and the author of several Motorbooks how-to titles, including *How to Build a Hot Rod*; *How to Plate, Polish, and Chrome*; *How to Restore and Customize Auto Upholstery and Interiors*; and *How to Paint Your Car*. He lives near St. Louis, Missouri.

CONTENTS

FOREWORD

You are lucky. When I started doing auto bodywork, I did not have a book like this to help me. My knowledge came from what I learned as I worked and what I learned by asking questions from professional auto body technicians I knew. This was a costly and time-consuming way to master a new skill. Dennis has prepared a lot of information for you to eliminate much of the learning by trial and error. You have a great head start, one which I did not have.

Do not be afraid to start an auto body project, but try to pick a small repair for your first experience. If you do make a mistake, you will be out some additional expense and the extra time that it will take to redo your work, but you will have learned something. Auto bodywork is a skill learned by doing. Dennis will prepare you with his book, but you need actual hands-on experiences to acquire the skill. As you do more bodywork, you will get faster and better, but everyone begins with that first job.

A completed auto body repair can bring a feeling of great satisfaction. My goal is to repair the vehicle so that the prior damage is undetectable by anyone. A custom or street rod job should be better than the standards of an original equipment manufacturer. The body and paint should be smooth, flat, and glossy, and all the body panels should fit as perfectly as possible. Set your standard very high and avoid the attitude that substandard work will be okay. After each job, critique your work. Make a mental note of what looks good and what you need to do better next time. In auto bodywork, each successive step depends on quality work done on the prior stage. A great paint job will not look good on substandard bodywork. Do each step of the process to the best of your ability, with the tools, skills, and the knowledge you have. Enjoy your auto body experiences. Take pride in your work and take credit for it. Nothing matches the feeling of hearing someone say, "Wow, you did all that work yourself? It looks great."

John Kimbrough

ACKNOWLEDGMENTS

A very sincere "thank you" goes out to everyone who helped with this book, as I could not have done it without you. In no particular order, thanks again to Jim Miller, Duane Wissman, and the staff at Jerry's Auto Body; Donnie and Jack Karg at Karg's Hot Rod Service; Keith Moritz and staff at Morfab Customs; along with Kevin and Wendy Brinkley at The Paint Store.

I also need to thank Roger Ward at Bad Paint Company and John Kimbrough for all of the information they have provided over the years and for the proofreading they have done on my manuscripts.

Dennis W. Parks

INTRODUCTION

Even if you are not a hot rodder, "car guy," or any other type of automobile aficionado, there are times when doing automotive bodywork yourself may present itself. Suppose your recently licensed teenager has just had a fender bender. You could claim it on your insurance and have the repair work done at your local body shop. However, you have to ask yourself, "What will this do to my insurance rates?" Or, maybe being a prudent parent, you have bought this first-time driver a relatively cheap vehicle and just carry liability insurance on it. The car runs well, but just isn't socially acceptable to your "image is everything" teenager. Depending on the amount of damage, you may not be able to pass the car off as brand-new, but with a little bit of work, you can probably make it look better. In the worst case, you will at least develop a better understanding of why auto body repair shops charge what they do.

Of course, if you are a car guy or gal, you may realize that the car of your dreams in perfect condition is beyond your means, but that you can have what you really want if you can restore or modify one that is in less-than-perfect condition. Starting out with a rusted out or dented hulk of a body and then transforming it into the vehicle of your dreams takes patience and passion, but when it is completed, it will mean more to you than an already finished vehicle that you have bought from someone else.

There is also the possibility of finding a vehicle that is in good shape mechanically, but needs some tender loving care in the bodywork department. If you can learn to hammer out a few dents and touch up some paint, you can often make some good money buying used cars, doing some minor bodywork, and then selling them. This scenario works very well if you live in or near a college town where decent-looking used vehicles for sale are in short supply.

Through the years, automobile construction has changed immensely and so have the ways in which cars are repaired. Although auto body repair at one time centered around hammering out dents in sheet-metal panels, it has now become largely a paint-and-replace industry as many of the components are made of composites that are cheaper to swap than to repair. Still, for many of us, repairing it ourselves is more desirable for any number of reasons.

It is the goal of this book to teach you how to make the necessary repairs to your bodywork, whether the panel to be repaired is metal or a composite. Chapters 1 and 2 will discuss the necessary tools and materials for performing auto body repair, while Chapter 3 will help you develop a strategy for making the repairs. By Chapter 4 we'll be getting our hands dirty by disassembling the vehicle as required and determining how best to strip old paint and rust from parts that need repair. Chapter 5 will discuss repairs to metal components, while Chapter 6 will deal primarily with composite body panels and their repair. Rust repair will be the prime subject for Chapter 7, while Chapters 8 and 9 will focus on post-repair surface preparation and paint application, respectively. Chapter 10 will finish up with the reassembly process.

I hope this book gets you motivated about performing your own auto body repair and gives you the confidence to do it yourself. You can save thousands—and maybe make thousands—by teaching yourself this valuable skill. Thank you for buying this book. May it serve you well as you turn eyesores into eye candy.

CHAPTER 1
TOOLS

No matter what the task may be, having the correct tools for the job will undoubtedly make the job easier and yield a better result. However, working on your own vehicle in your own garage doesn't require you to have every tool that the local body shop owns. For a professional body shop, time is money, so it makes sense for the shop to invest in costly tools that can speed up the process and pay for themselves over time. You won't need to have the latest widget to do your own bodywork, but the basic tools you do acquire should be high quality items that will do their job well and serve you for many years.

BASIC TOOLS

There are certain basic tools that are necessary, whether you do the work as a profession or as a hobby. These are hammers, dollies, sanding boards, grinders, and sanders. You cannot really do much bodywork if you do not have these basic tools. Spray guns for applying primer and paint are basic as well, but are listed with the pneumatic tools. Besides, this is a book about bodywork. For priming and painting, you can refer to *How to Paint Your Car* by David H. Jacobs and Dennis W. Parks.

These are some of the basic tools required for automotive bodywork. Beginning at the upper left is a cheese grater file, a slide hammer, a small sanding block, a lead file, a long sanding board, a body hammer, and a dolly.

Body hammers come in a variety of shapes, sizes, and uses. Those with a serrated head are used for shrinking metal. Round heads are used for general panel flattening, while square heads are used for restoring bodylines.

Hammers

Leading the list of basic tools are hammers—and you must admit hammers are pretty basic. However, there are a variety of hammers that are used for bodywork and they all have their specific characteristics and applications. There are situations that call for a big hammer and others that call for a smaller hammer and a lighter touch. Learning to know the difference between the two will take some time, but with experience you'll know exactly which one you need for any given job.

Most body hammers have a head and a pick, making it a dual-purpose tool. The head is usually large (between 1 and 2 inches in diameter) and relatively flat with a smooth surface, while the pick end is much smaller and pointed. The larger head is used for flattening metal against a dolly. For more detail on this technique, refer to the section titled Dolly-On/Dolly-Off Hammering, in Chapter 5. The pick end is typically used for hammering out very small, localized dents, with or without a dolly. Picks can come to a very narrow point or to more of a blunt point.

When sheet metal is bent in a collision, in addition to bending, it stretches. To reduce some of this stretching, a shrinking hammer is used. Shrinking hammers are similar to other hammers, except that the head is serrated.

Different hammer manufacturers combine different heads with different picks. If you purchase a set that contains a flat face, a shrinking face, a blunt pick, and a sharp pointed pick, it will fulfill most of your hammering needs.

Mallets

Mallets differ from bodywork hammers in construction material and shape, as well as use. The striking surface is usually made of plastic or some other composite that will not mar sheet metal or aluminum. Mallets are available in different sizes and may be cylindrical or teardrop shaped. While hammers are typically used to return damaged auto body sheet metal to a preformed shape, mallets are generally used to hammer flat sheet metal into a custom shape.

Mallets are typically used for hammer-forming flat sheet metal into custom shapes and sometimes require a wooden buck to hammer the metal against.

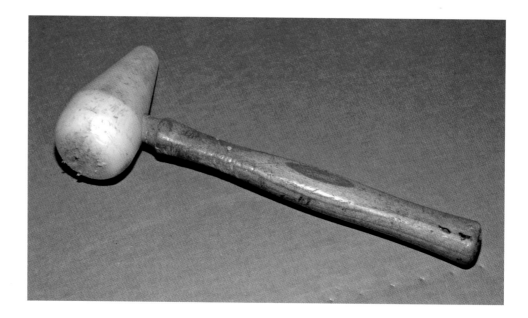

Just like hammers, dollies come in a variety of shapes and sizes. A wider variety of shapes will enable you to recreate original bodylines more precisely. At the upper left is a toe dolly with increasing and decreasing radii, at right is a general purpose dolly with a variety of shapes, and at the bottom is a serrated dolly for shrinking metal.

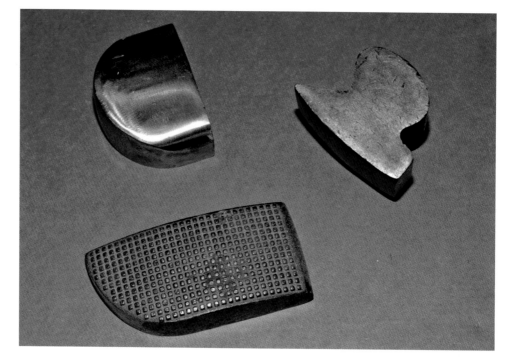

Dollies

Made of hardened steel that has been smoothed, dollies come in a variety of shapes and sizes. Dollies are usually held on the back side of the metal being straightened, while a hammer on the outside flattens the panel between the two, resulting in metal that is roughly the shape of the portion of the dolly being used. For this reason, a variety of dollies with small, large, convex, and concave shapes will give you some versatility. Like shrinking hammers, dollies with a serrated face will help to shrink stretched metal.

Spoons

For use inside hard-to-reach areas, spoons are much like a body dolly with a handle. Typically smaller and thinner than a dolly, they can be used inside of doors, fenders, hoods, or other double wall panels. Spoons can also be used for prying panels outward.

Sanding Blocks and Boards

Sanding blocks are commercially available in a very wide variety of shapes, styles, sizes, and materials, while

With its serrated surface, a shrinking dolly (shown) or shrinking hammer can be used to shrink metal that has been stretched in a collision. Hammering the metal against, or with, the serrated surface causes the material to bunch up, thereby shrinking its surface area.

improvised sanding blocks are pretty much unlimited. No matter how good you may be at straightening damaged sheet metal, unless you expend the required effort to get the surface both smooth and flat, the finished paint simply will not look its best. Skillful sanding allows for a nice paint job, while sanding without the aid of a sanding block is merely a waste of your time. No matter how smooth the body may feel, without use of a sanding block it will look wavy and unprofessional with paint on it.

Sanding blocks enable you to exert even pressure on the sandpaper so that you can minimize waves in the sanded surface. Since automotive body panels come in a variety of contours, there are different requirements for sanding blocks. If the panel has lots of curves or round surfaces, the sanding block needs to be flexible but firm to maintain contact between the body surface and the sandpaper. Flexible sanding blocks are made out of rubber or various

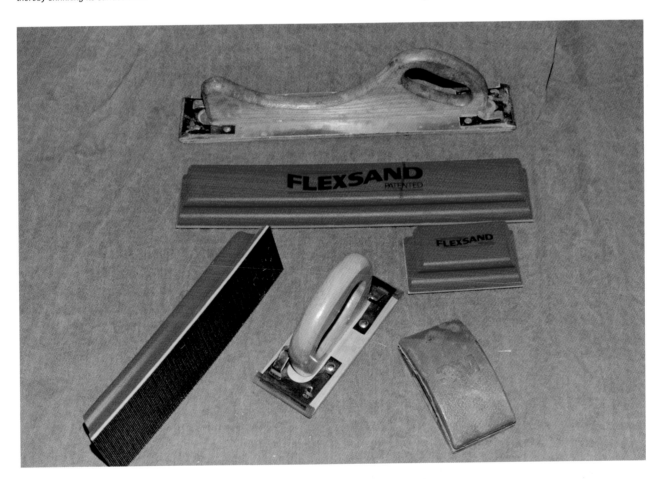

These are just a few of the many types and sizes of sanding boards. The three Flexsand boards are about the middle of the road, in terms of stiffness, and secure the sandpaper with hook-and-loop backing. The two sanding boards with hardwood handles are the stiffest and therefore are best for large flat surfaces. They secure the sandpaper with a spring clip. The small rubber block at the lower right is the most flexible. Sandpaper fits into a slot on each end and is secured with a couple of tacks that are part of the block.

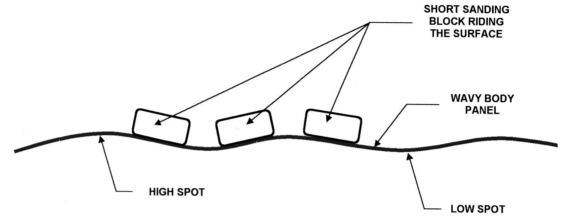

SHORT SANDING
BLOCK RIDING
THE SURFACE

WAVY BODY
PANEL

HIGH SPOT

LOW SPOT

Besides smoothing the surface, sanding makes wavy panels flat. A short sanding board or block can be used to get any panel smooth, but will not necessarily get the panel flat. It will merely ride over the ridges, rather than knocking them down.

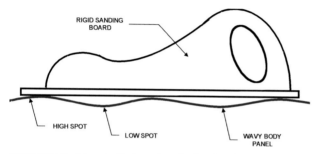

RIGID SANDING
BOARD

HIGH SPOT

LOW SPOT

WAVY BODY
PANEL

On the other hand, by using the longest sanding board possible for the area being sanded, you can get the sandpaper to span across the ridges in a body panel, and it will quickly knock down the ridges, making the panel flat as well as smooth.

types of foam. Some sanding blocks may be fine-tuned for flexibility through the use of removable rods: add rods to stiffen the block or remove rods to make it more flexible.

On the other hand, if you are sanding a flat surface (such as a hood or roof panel), a more rigid sanding board would be appropriate. The more rigid and longer the board, the more effective it will be in eliminating waves in the panel. A longer board will span across multiple ripples, working to knock down the high spots, whereas a short sanding block will merely follow the waves without eliminating them.

Although most sanding blocks and boards have a flat surface, some sanding boards are designed with a concave surface, allowing you to smooth the inside of a curved surface. These are available in a variety of radii.

Whenever you purchase sanding boards or blocks, you should take special notice of how the sandpaper is held in place, as not all sandpaper is compatible with all sanding boards and blocks. Small inexpensive rubber sanding blocks often have a horizontal slit in both ends, with the

top flap having two or three sharp tacks that grab the sandpaper. The sandpaper is wrapped around the bottom of the block, and the ends of the paper are placed between the upper and lower flap and held in place by the tacks. Some sanding boards have spring clips that hold the paper in place. Still others use adhesive-backed sandpaper.

Portable Grinders and Sanders

For most do-it-yourself repairs, sending a panel to be media blasted or chemically stripped isn't feasible. So for quickly removing paint, primer, and old body filler from an area to be repaired, a sander or grinder is a must. These are available in electric or pneumatic models, as well as in different sizes, motor speeds, and price ranges.

If you do not own an air compressor, you should purchase an electric sander, as your shop is most likely within extension cord reach of an electric outlet. If you already have an air compressor that can maintain a large volume of air, a pneumatic model may be more appropriate. A pneumatic model will be able to withstand longer non-stop use, while an electric model will get hot after a while, causing the motor to shut down. Pressing the reset switch will usually allow it to start again, but this can become more of an inconvenience as the work progresses.

For working in large areas, a larger sanding surface will be better, but will be limited by smaller areas. This author has had good luck owning both a smaller, high-speed grinder and a larger, slower-speed sander. Both can be equipped with sanding discs for removing paint. The relatively small grinder (around 4 inches) can be equipped with a grinding disc for work on heavy metal such as chassis, while the 7-inch sander can be equipped with a polishing bonnet for buffing and polishing operations.

At the lower left is a 4¹/₂-inch Makita grinder that can use a rigid grinding disc for grinding welds. It will also accept a wire cup brush, which is useful for removing old body filler or paint. The larger unit is a 7-inch Craftsman sander/buffer. With sanding discs of various grits, it can be used to clean welds or remove old paint or body filler. It can also be fitted with a buffing bonnet to apply wax to finished paint.

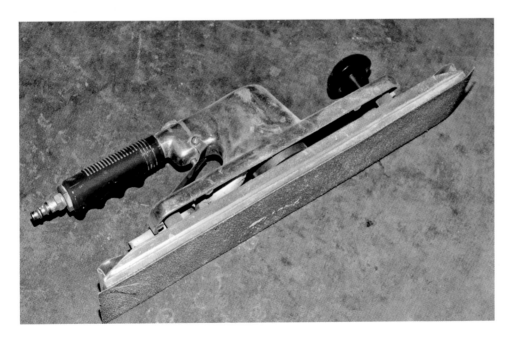

Pneumatic sanding boards that move in a straight line are very useful for block sanding body filler to get it flat. However, they should not be used for removing paint or surface rust; an orbital sander/grinder is more effective.

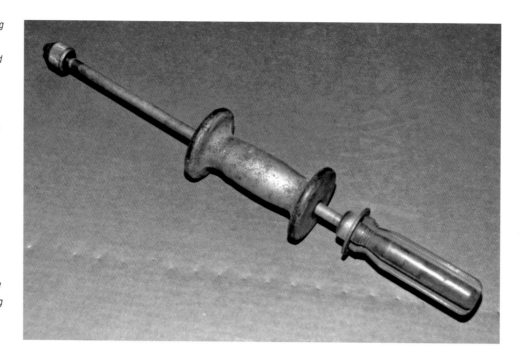

A slide hammer is used for pulling out dents in sheet metal. In the past, small screws were threaded into tiny holes drilled into the sheet metal, whereas most body shops now use a stud gun that quickly spot-welds a metal pin to the sheet metal. In either case, you should tighten the small end of the slide hammer onto the screw or pin. With one hand on the handle and the other hand on the hammer (sliding portion), slide the hammer back into the handle in a quick motion, with the raps on the handle pulling the sheet metal out as if it were being hammered on from the inside.

Stud Welders and Slide Hammers

For pulling out dents in sheet metal, the electric stud welder has made repair work much easier than past methods. A stud welder spot-welds a metal pin to the sheet-metal panel. The more complex the dent, the more pins need to be used.

After the pins are installed, a slide hammer is clamped onto a pin located in the deepest part of the dent. The pin is then pulled outward by sliding the cylindrical hammer outward quickly along the shaft of the slide hammer. By pulling each of the pins outward using this method, the sheet metal will begin to move back into its original shape. The pins are then cut off and other methods of bodywork (hammer and dolly, body filler, etc.) are performed to complete the repair.

This slide hammer technique has been used for quite some time; however, before stud welders, it was a complicated process. Small holes would be drilled into the sheet metal, and then a screw threaded partially into the hole. After the slide hammer was used to pull the dent, a bunch of small holes would be left in the repaired panel. These would weaken the panel, become a starting point for rust, and they would need to be welded shut. Without an electric stud welder, using a slide hammer often created more problems than it solved.

Door Skin Installer and Removal Pliers

Manufacturers typically hold door skins in place by folding the edge of the outer door skin (sheet metal) over the edge of the inner door structure. The skin is then spot-welded in place. This process makes door skins easy to remove and replace, but having the correct tools sure beats improvising. To remove the skin, a body worker drills out the spot welds and then pries the sheet metal away from the door frame. This can be done with a pry bar or a screwdriver, but using specially designed door skin removal pliers speeds up the process and makes it much easier. At around 30 bucks, these pliers will pay for themselves in time savings after just a few doors.

Conversely, door skin installer pliers are designed to fold the edge of the door skin over the door frame. These pliers are more expensive, but they create a more uniform fold and don't dent the door skin as a hammer would do.

Panel Flangers

The ability to create a flange on a piece of sheet metal is useful any time when you are attaching two panels to one another. Rather than simply butting the edges of the two panels together, creating a flange in one piece allows that piece to fit behind the second piece, yet still have an edge to abut. The two pieces can then be plug welded together or attached with rivets, depending on the application. If the panels are merely riveted together, you should use steel rivets in steel panels and aluminum rivets in aluminum panels. Panel flanging tools are available in two basic styles: as a bead roller through which the sheet metal is fed, or as clamping pliers that are used manually. The bead roller style includes inexpensive models that clamp into a bench vise and stand-alone units. Price will depend on whether the metal is fed

Left: *A bead roller can be used to roll beads or to flange panels, depending on the shape of the mandrels. This particular example clamps into a bench mounted vise and is cranked by hand (rather than having a drive motor).*

Below: *This is the resultant rolled bead. Note that this raised portion is what would be on the underneath side of the metal as it goes through the bead roller. You can therefore roll beads that protrude or recess on the finished panel, depending on which way the metal is inserted through the roller.*

Left: *These mandrels are used to roll a bead in the sheet metal. The metal is inserted between these two rollers and the metal fed by rotating the crank at the opposite end of the roller shafts. As the sheet metal is fed through, it takes on the shape of the mandrel, in this case a rolled bead.*

by hand crank or motor and the thickness of metal that the tool can handle. Regardless of style or size, the sheet metal is fed between two mandrels that are each mounted to the end of two long cylinders. The shape of the machined mandrels is what gives the sheet metal its new shape. Each flanging mandrel has two different size diameters, which is what creates the flange. A bead mandrel would work the same way, but one mandrel would have a cylindrical shape with a convex ring around it near the end. The mating mandrel to this would have a concave ring that aligns with the convex ring, resulting in a raised bead in the sheet metal.

Manual flangers operate much like locking pliers. The heads of the pliers are stepped (similar to the flanging mandrel), which creates a flange when the sheet metal is clamped between the jaws of the pliers. This style requires flanging the sheet metal in one location, releasing the pliers, moving them along the edge to be flanged, and then flanging again. If you have lots of flanges to make, this will take longer, but it is much cheaper than the bead roller.

PNEUMATIC TOOLS

Other than spraying primer and paint, most anything that can be done with pneumatic tools can be done with the basic hand operated tools listed previously. However, using air-powered tools will speed up the process and therefore leave more time for more detailed finish work if you are so

Pneumatic tools need plenty of compressed air. This commercial unit requires 240-volt electric service and has about a 60-gallon air tank. For use in your home garage, you may be better off finding a 110-volt unit, unless you have extra electric service installed. Whichever you choose, get the largest tank you can afford and for which you have room.

inclined. It will also no doubt leave you less fatigued at the end of a work session.

You must realize, though, that just because you are using power tools, this doesn't mean that the task is going to turn out better. If you don't know what you are doing, using a pneumatic sander or grinder will get you into trouble a whole lot faster than if you were sanding by hand. You should also realize that the speed and ease of pneumatic tools comes with a price. If you are an automotive hobbyist, the price might be reasonable, especially if you foresee other automotive projects in your future. If you are simply trying to make a one-time repair, you may be better off buying or borrowing the necessary hand tools to make the repair . . . even if it means having the paint work done by Maaco or some other re-paint shop.

Air Compressors

Most professional paint shops use an air compressor that is rated at a minimum of 10 horsepower and often have even larger compressors. These are big units that supply plenty of air for the operation of pneumatic tools and some painting equipment simultaneously. For the hobbyist, a smaller compressor may be satisfactory, as long as the compressor is rated at 4 horsepower or greater and has a tank that is at least 25 gallons.

Horsepower is not the only important criterion for an air compressor; equally if not more important is the size of the tank. The more a compressor works, the hotter the air supply becomes. As heat continues to be generated, moisture is introduced into the air system through condensation inside piping. You want your air compressor to build up a reserve of compressed air in its holding tank, and then shut off for a while to cool down.

The best way to determine what size air compressor will meet your needs is to compare the cfm of air your pneumatic tools will require to the cfm rating on the compressor you plan to use. If the compressor can easily supply the required cfm at the prescribed application pressure, you should have no problem.

Your compressor must also have an adequate capacity. As an example, a 5-horsepower compressor with a 20-gallon tank that supplies enough air for a conventional spray gun may not be able to keep up with the demands of a high volume, low pressure (HVLP) spray gun. Instead of being able to spray a complete coat of paint at one time, you may have to stop in the middle (or several times) to allow the air supply to catch up. The same 5-horsepower compressor with a 35-gallon tank may be more appropriate when using an HVLP. Likewise, when using other high demand pneumatic tools, such as a plasma cutter or sander, a larger capacity tank will prevent the need to stop in the middle of the task to let the air compressor catch up with you.

Hoses and Couplings

A factor that could cause false pressure gauge readings is the size of the air hose used to supply your air tools. Small-diameter hoses will experience friction loss and cause pressures to dwindle when the air travels from the air compressor to the tool being powered. PPG's *Refinish Manual* suggests that a $1/4$-inch hose is too small for standard production paint guns. It recommends a $5/16$-inch inside-diameter hose in maximum lengths of 25 feet. For HVLP spray guns, a $3/8$-inch inside-diameter air hose is recommended. As long as you are using compatible hoses and couplings and have a compressor of sufficient size, the larger the diameter of the

Pressure regulators are essential between the air compressor and the tool being used. This particular model has an air supply line entering from the right and is used to regulate two separate lines that exit from the left. Sanders, grinders, and air saws require a certain amount of air to operate properly, while spray guns must be operated within a specific air pressure range depending on the material being applied.

air hose, the better. Except for some used with a commercial quality sand blaster, most air hoses found in a body repair paint shop will be 1-inch diameter or less.

Regulators

To ensure that you have the recommended air pressure for your air tools, hold the trigger wide open while adjusting the air pressure regulator controls. Although a control gauge setting might show 40 psi while in a static condition, operating your air tools may cause it to drop down to 30 or 35 psi. Most pneumatic tools are designed to work most efficiently at a particular airflow rate that will vary from one piece of equipment to another. If your air compressor cannot provide enough air, most tools will simply not be as efficient as you would like. Even so, it is important to apply auto paint at the psi rating indicated on the container label or in the product's application guide literature.

Driers/Filters

One cannot overemphasize the importance of a clean, dry, and controlled source of pressurized air for any spray paint job (yes, this applies to primer as well). If moisture is allowed to accumulate and eventually exit a spray gun's nozzle, the paint finish will be blemished with fish eyes, dirt nibs, and possibly blushing problems all over the surface. Miniscule particles of water, oil, or rust will find their way from holding tanks to other air-powered tools as well, unless they are captured and retained somewhere between the compressor and equipment being used.

You could buy the most expensive auto paint products, spend weeks and weeks preparing your car or truck's surface to perfection, use the most highly advanced spray paint gun available, and then *ruin* your paint job by relying upon an inadequate air compressor or a holding tank loaded with moisture and oil residue. You can also ruin your other pneumatic tools if they are allowed to intake moist air, as this may cause the internal components to rust, greatly shortening their useful life.

After you have figured out which air compressor to use, consider the installation of a piping system with a water trap or air drier located at the end. Even for home use, a small air supply system with $^3/_4$- to 1-inch pipe could be advantageous. A copper or galvanized pipe running downhill away from a compressor toward a water trap or dryer will allow moisture accumulations in heated air to flow away from the compressor and toward the trap or dryer. Since the hot air will have time to cool inside pipes, moisture suspended in the air will condense into droplets that can be captured and retained as a liquid in the trap.

Do-it-yourself body hobbyists can run $^3/_4$- to 1-inch copper or galvanized pipe up from their compressor location to the ceiling, then attach a horizontal section to the riser and run it slightly downhill toward the opposite end of the garage or workshop. Another section can then run down the wall to a convenient point where a water trap or air dryer can be mounted. Working air lines can connect at the trap or dryer to be used for pneumatic tools or spray guns.

To keep portable air compressors mobile and to prevent their operational vibration from causing damage to solid piping mounted to walls, it is recommended that you connect your compressor to your piping system with a short, flexible air hose. By doing this, you can easily disconnect

To the left is a conventional siphon-feed spray gun, while the one on the right is a high volume, low pressure (HVLP) model. They were purchased new for around 100 bucks each, although they were on the inexpensive end of the spectrum. Unless you are painting vehicles on a daily basis, either of these would probably suit your purposes.

the air compressor from the piping system to move it to wherever it's needed for other kinds of jobs.

Spray Guns

Even if you have no intention of actually applying paint, applying primers and other substrates will be required during the bodywork repair stage. This will require a spray gun, which can be purchased in a variety of designs over a very broad price range.

Before purchasing a spray gun, you should determine if you will be using traditional paint products (solvent-based) or the new waterborne paints. Now before you get alarmed about waterborne paint products, you must realize that they are not mandatory everywhere and are difficult to obtain in areas where they are not required. Waterborne paint has been a requirement in portions of Europe for some time and is becoming a requirement in California. However, the general consensus is that waterborne paints will not be required outside of these restricted areas until around the end of the first quarter of the twenty-first century (2025).

Other than the possibility of requiring different air pressures, waterborne paints are applied just like solvent-based paints. The difference in the spray gun is that waterborne-compatible spray guns utilize stainless steel or other materials that won't rust. Again, unless you are in an area that currently requires the use of waterborne paint, you most likely will not be affected by this for another 20 or so years. Throughout the rest of this book, methods and equipment will apply to both solvent-based and waterborne paint, unless specifically designated as one or the other.

HVLP

Along with waterborne paint that eliminates most, if not all, solvents and the related volatile organic compounds (VOC) that are associated with paint products, the advent of HVLP spray guns has arguably been the biggest recent advance in auto repair. Just as the name implies, these spray guns deliver the paint by using higher volume of air at lower pressure than conventional spray guns. Anyone who has used a conventional spray gun knows the cloud of overspray they produce. This overspray is the result of the paint material bouncing off the surface since it is being applied at such high pressure. Lower pressure application keeps more paint on the surface, consumes less material, and reduces pollution and cleanup.

Conventional (Suction Feed)

Conventional or suction-feed spray guns are slowly but surely disappearing from the marketplace. Their design calls for higher air pressure to pull the paint from the cup and propel it toward the surface to be painted. This high air pressure causes much of the paint to bounce off the surface and results in non-efficient overspray. Although suction feed guns can give excellent results, HVLP guns apply the paint much more efficiently.

Conventional guns became less expensive with the advent of HVLP spray guns, however, the latter can now be found for similar prices. The amount of material saved when using HVLP versus a conventional gun will quickly make up for any additional cost in equipment purchase.

To the left is a conventional siphon spray gun alongside a much smaller detail (or jamb) gun. The larger gun has a 1-quart capacity cup and is used to apply primer or paint to large areas. The detail gun is used to apply primer or paint to small areas or, more commonly, confined areas where a full-size gun would be difficult to maneuver.

Full Size

Full-size spray guns are designed for use when applying primer or paint to large areas, such as a fender, door, or the entire vehicle. They can be either HVLP or suction-feed and typically have a paint cup that holds about a quart or liter of sprayable material. Full-size spray guns can be used to spray substrates, such as primer, or topcoats, such as paint or clear.

Fluid Tip Sizes

The size of the fluid tip is what determines the type of material that can be sprayed through a spray gun and the air pressure required to do so. Primers and other substrates are typically thicker than topcoats (paint and clear), while heavy coatings (such as bed liner material) are thicker still. These thick materials require a fluid tip of about 2.2 millimeters in size, while primer can be sprayed through a fluid tip that is between 1.5 and 1.8 millimeters. Basecoats and clear can usually be sprayed with fluid tips between 1.2 and 1.5 millimeters in size.

When purchasing a spray gun, select a tip that is compatible for what you will be spraying. Most spray guns have removable fluid tips, although some may be sold with just one size tip included, while others include different size fluid tips. If you are going to be doing a lot of bodywork and painting, you would probably be better off purchasing one gun for spraying primer and another for spraying topcoats. If you are doing a one-time project, one spray gun with multiple tips might serve your purposes.

Detail

Detail spray guns are also known as jamb guns as they are particularly suited for spraying in confined areas such as doorjambs. They can be used to spray primer or topcoats. Their paint cup is much smaller than that of a full-size spray gun, so using a detail gun for painting or priming an entire panel would require filling the paint cup several times.

CUTTING TOOLS

Prior to installing a patch panel in sheet metal, it is necessary to cut out the area that is being replaced, whether the damage is from rust, severe collision, or some other reason. If the rusty sheet metal is not removed, the rust will simply expand to the new sheet metal. Damaged sheet metal must be removed in order to get the replacement to fit correctly.

Air Chisel

For removing rivets or stripped bolts in chassis or other heavy metal quickly and easily, air chisels work great. They can also be used to quickly cut through sheet metal, such as when removing a quarter panel prior to installation of a new panel. These consume lots of air, so if you intend to make regular use of an air chisel, buy or rent a larger capacity air compressor for the best results. If you haven't purchased the chisel or compressor, check the air chisel's requirements first.

Die Grinder

For making relatively straight cuts in sheet metal, a die grinder with a cut-off wheel works very well. Most com-

This is a pneumatic die grinder that can be employed to make straight cuts in metal. It is typically used as a cut-off tool for small material or to cut out old metal where a patch panel will be installed. Prices range from less than $50 up to about $100.

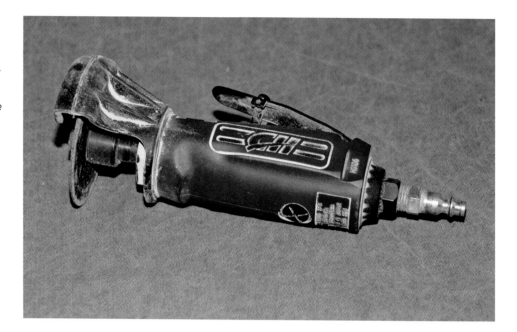

An angle head grinder works the same as an ordinary die grinder, but with its angled head, it can sometimes get into areas where an ordinary die grinder cannot, depending on how flexible the air hose may be.

mercially available patch panels have straight edges, so using a die grinder allows you to cut out a similar shape quite easily. Be sure to leave about $1/2$ inch of the old metal to overlap the patch panel, and the new panel can be plug welded in place quite easily.

Although they operate the same and perform the same task, die grinders are available in two distinctly different configurations. In both types, the air hose attaches to the end of the die grinder's body, the body serves as the handle when in use, and a lever type trigger is squeezed against the body to operate it. The difference in the two styles is that the grinding wheel rotates perpendicular to the body of one type of die grinder, while the grinding head is mounted at 90 degrees to the body on the other. If you have plenty of room in your workspace, this is not a big deal, but when space is limited, a die grinder with the angled head will usually be more maneuverable.

Reciprocating Air Saw

For anyone who has used a jigsaw or a scroll saw for woodworking, the reciprocating air saw is roughly the equivalent for sheet metal. Having a blade that moves back and forth, it can cut curves or straight cuts in sheet metal, therefore offering more versatility than a die grinder. It is typically used for cutting metal that is still attached to the vehicle, such as when removing rusted or damaged areas that will be replaced with a patch panel.

Shears

Bench mounted or portable, metal shears work much the same way as scissors—two or more blades acting against each other, cutting the metal in the process. A long arm and ratchet or gear mechanism works to ease the process of cutting sheet metal. Shears are often used for cutting custom patch panels from a piece of flat sheet metal prior to it being welded to the vehicle.

Nibblers

Nibblers are usually hand operated (much like scissors) and therefore are limited to thinner sheet metal than shears. They feature a compound leverage mechanism, making them quick and easy to use, as long as you stay within their limits.

Plasma Cutter

Powered by a combination of compressed air and electricity, plasma cutters can be used to cut almost anything, although they are not suitable for cutting through multiple layers of material at one time. The only limiting factor is the thickness and that varies depending on model and material being cut. Plasma cutters have a cutting head that resembles a metal inert gas (MIG) welding torch; you simply place the head on the material to be cut, squeeze the trigger, and then pull the head along the line to be

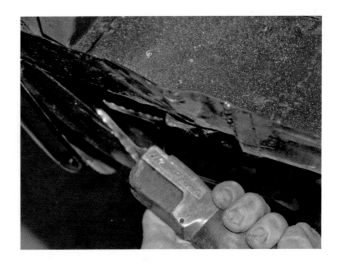

A narrow, replaceable blade makes a reciprocating air saw a good tool for making free-form cuts in sheet metal.

TOOLS

cut. Plasma cutters can be used freehand, but they provide a more precise cut if you follow some sort of pattern. A word of caution: plasma cutters use an incredibly hot arc to melt the material they are cutting, allowing them to cut virtually anything, including fingers.

A plasma cutter is used much like how a cutting torch was used in the past. The main difference is that the plasma cutter provides a much more precise arc. This minimizes the amount of "finish" work that is required after the initial work of cutting is completed. A cutting torch may still be usable on occasion, especially for doing the rough amputation of a portion of a chassis or quarter panel from a donor vehicle. When the final cutting to size is done, however, a plasma cutter will provide more accurate cuts.

These are compound leverage snips, which are commonly known as aviation snips. They are used to cut free-form shapes in light metal. The green handled pair is designed to cut straight or toward the right, while the red handled pair is designed to cut straight or toward the left. The yellow pair in the middle is designed to cut straight only.

Requiring electric power, an electric ground, and a good supply of dry, compressed air, a plasma arc cutter will cut virtually anything. Larger, more expensive units can cut thicker materials, while relatively inexpensive units can cut sheet metal and other materials up to about 1/4 inch thick quite handily.

When using a plasma cutter or welder around glass (or flammable materials), you should use a welding curtain. Sparks of any kind can damage glass or ignite flammable materials.

Panel Flangers

Although they may be too expensive for you to purchase for a one-time collision repair, many professional shops have pneumatic panel flangers. At least one type of pneumatic panel flanger also punches holes in sheet metal, which is very useful if you are going to be plug welding panels together.

STAND-ALONE TOOLS

The following stand-alone tools are more commonly found in shops where professional or serious amateurs do bodywork. Some items are expensive while others are pretty reasonable. You won't need them for every task, but there is no doubt that having them makes the job easier.

Welders

For permanently joining two or more pieces of metal, welding is the overall best option. It isn't the only way, as rivets have been around for years. However, rivets can vibrate loose, making them less desirable for automotive applica-

When plug welding an item such as a patch panel, one panel must have a small hole in it prior to every weld. Rather than drilling each hole, this pneumatic panel flanger punches a hole at a press of the lever.

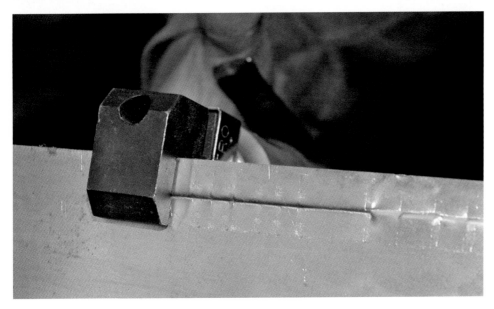

Left: In similar fashion, this pneumatic panel flanger also presses a flange when you insert the sheet metal into the opposite side of the head and press the operating lever. This method may take longer than using a bead rolling flanger, but it is more versatile in accessibility.

Below: After just a minute or two with the pneumatic flanger, both of these pieces of sheet metal have been flanged, allowing them to be aligned and welded together more easily.

tions. Most automotive body metal is steel or aluminum, which can be welded with either MIG or tungsten inert gas (TIG) welding. Stainless steel, copper, or brass can also be welded with either method. MIG welding is undoubtedly easier to learn, while TIG welding provides the highest quality and the most aesthetic weld beads. For more information regarding welders and welding, refer to MBI's *How to Weld: Techniques and Tips for Beginners and Pros* by Todd Bridigum.

MIG

For welding patch panels in place, MIG welders are ideal. They are easy to learn to use properly, are more

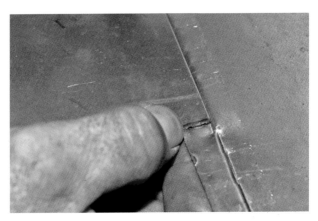

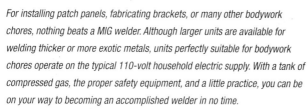

For installing patch panels, fabricating brackets, or many other bodywork chores, nothing beats a MIG welder. Although larger units are available for welding thicker or more exotic metals, units perfectly suitable for bodywork chores operate on the typical 110-volt household electric supply. With a tank of compressed gas, the proper safety equipment, and a little practice, you can be on your way to becoming an accomplished welder in no time.

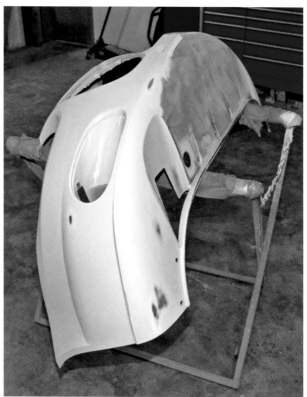

For doing any kind of work on a fender, door, or in this case a front fascia/bumper assembly, a folding work stand is very beneficial. It is typically much easier to fill, sand, and paint while you are standing up, rather than lying on the ground. You can find these at swap meets for around $25 or through tool supply stores for a little more. For temporary or one-time use, you could easily make your own out of any kind of tubing that you have lying around.

than adequate for sheet-metal work, and are affordable. Many models require only 115 volts, making them great for home use. These single-phase models can typically weld up to $^3/_8$-inch-thick metal, which is more than adequate for most auto body repairs. Larger models that require three-phase electric service are used mainly in production or fabrication shops, or in applications that require welding metal that is thicker than $^3/_8$ inch.

Some additional benefits of MIG welding are relatively high-speed welding, good control on thin metals, and very little weld splatter. Although you will need to skip around some to avoid warping the metal due to heat buildup, being able to lay down a great deal of weld bead in a short time will save you time on a repair. The ability to control the heat allows thorough weld penetration without burning through relatively thin sheet-metal body panels. Little to no weld splatter means less cleanup prior to adding body filler or primer/paint applications.

TIG

TIG welding is more suitable for heavy chassis fabrication or repair than it is for light sheet-metal work. It is certainly more difficult to learn but, in the hands of an experienced welder, can yield a beautiful weld that needs little if any cleanup afterward.

TIG welding can be used to weld titanium or magnesium alloys. Not that you are going to be welding these types of material on a daily basis, but a MIG welder will not be able to complete these tasks properly or as efficiently.

Locking clamps are very common in almost all body shops. These are being used to clamp the outer wheelhouse of an early Camaro to the newly replaced quarter panel.

On the downside of the MIG versus TIG debate, TIG is generally slower and requires more practice to master. However, once you master TIG welding, you can weld virtually any type of metal.

Work Stands

For many bodywork repairs, no panels are removed from the vehicle. However, if you are required to remove a door, fender, hood, deck lid, or bumper from the vehicle to repair that panel, having a work stand or workbench to sit it on will be a great benefit. It simply isn't practical to do bodywork on a fender while the fender is sitting on the garage floor. Whether you purchase a commercially available work stand or make your own, be sure to put some padding on it so you don't scratch or dent whatever you are working on.

Clamps

Bar clamps, spring clamps, locking pliers, and C-clamps all have their uses when you do bodywork. It would be impossible to itemize all of their uses, but when you need one or several, you will know it.

Infrared (IR) Heat Lamps

For the one-time repair, heat lamps are an expensive luxury. But, if you are pressed for time and need to dry primer or paint quickly, these will do the trick. They can also be used to accelerate the cure time of plastic body filler.

Shrinkers/Stretchers

These are commonly used for fabricating curved pieces of metal angle, such as windshield frames, wheelwell edges, and framework for trunk openings. They are usually pedestal mounted and can be manually or pneumatically operated.

THE COST OF TOOLS

Tools in general come in a very wide variety of qualities and purchase prices. Guys and gals who make their living with their bodywork and mechanic tools will usually buy only from Snap-On or another one of the expensive tool distributors that frequent the repair shops. These are no doubt high quality tools, but built into their price is the door-to-door service that accompanies them.

Many amateurs get by with less expensive tools. You can save money by doing so, but you do get what you pay for, so you'll get better and longer service if you avoid the cheapest stuff. Craftsman is a good mid-price tool and anything made in the United States is usually of good quality, though becoming harder to find. You can often judge quality by the tool's finish. If it looks cheap, it's probably not as strong. Cheap wrenches and screwdrivers break more easily, and cheap pliers are usually looser and harder to use precisely.

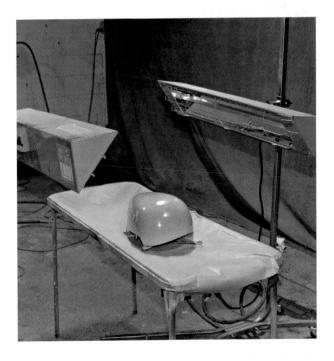

Although they are somewhat expensive to buy for the beginning body worker, infrared heat lamps can speed up the curing times for plastic filler or the drying process of paint. You must make sure that you do not speed up the process too much, but if you are pressed for time, these can help you out.

CHAPTER 2
MATERIALS

In addition to the hardware such as hammers, dollies, sanders, and welders used to straighten, smooth, and join metal, there are many other components to the bodywork equation. Some of these, such as paint stripper and body filler, can be applied by hand and require very few tools. The rest of these materials—the various primers and sealers that serve as a base for the final paint—are typically applied with a spray gun, which requires compressed air.

HAND APPLICATIONS

Most, if not all, of the products associated with auto body repair contain some type of solvent or other chemicals that can cause skin irritation, or worse, if your skin comes in direct contact with it. For this reason, it is imperative to read the warning labels of these materials prior to using them. Even if the warnings do not suggest wearing disposable gloves, it is a good practice to get into. Disposable gloves are very inexpensive and their use sure beats picking fiberglass resin or body filler from your fingers and cuticles.

Paint Stripper

Old paint can be removed from steel parts and some other metals with paint stripper. This type of product may not be suitable for use on all metals or finishes, so you should consult your paint supply jobber for their recommendations on which products to use. A particular brand that is commonly used for stripping paint from automobiles is Klean-Strip Aircraft Paint Remover.

Contrary to what many people believe, chemical stripping does not involve acid, it does involve a collection of chemicals that you must be careful with during use and disposal. Chemical paint strippers are safe to use, but you must respect them and follow the appropriate safety precautions to prevent burns or other skin irritations.

Wax and Grease Remover

Before sanding, priming, or painting any surface, that surface needs to be as clean as possible, with all traces of dirt, grease, oil, silicone, or other contaminants removed. If the surface is not clean prior to sanding, you run the risk of smearing any present contaminants onto a larger area and also further embedding them into the surface. If the sur-

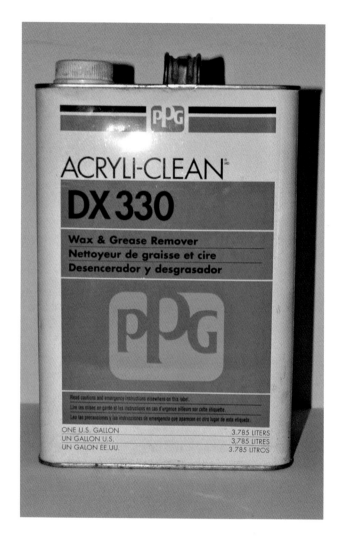

Body filler, primer, and paint will not adhere correctly to dirt, grease, oil, or other contaminated surfaces. To remove these contaminants, wipe or spray on wax and grease remover, and then wipe it off with another clean cloth or paper towel.

face is not clean prior to applying primer or paint, the freshly applied coating will not adhere properly. Even oil from your fingers is enough to deter proper adhesion, so avoid touching the surface with your bare hands.

To obtain this clean surface, you must use wax and grease remover. Wax and grease remover is readily available at your favorite paint supplier and is relatively inexpensive, so there is no reason to be without it. After using an air gun to blow away any dust or dirt, apply the wax and grease remover with a clean cloth (or paper towel) or spray it onto the surface. Wipe the surface dry, using a clean dry cloth (or paper towel). It should be apparent that the use of a clean cloth is of utmost importance here, as using any old shop towel that may have grease, brake fluid, or any other contaminants would be defeating the purpose.

Fiberglass

For custom work or bodywork repair, fiberglass is easy to learn to work with and does not require specialized equipment. Fiberglass can obviously be used to repair other fiberglass components, but it can also be used as an alternative to welding in sheet-metal patch panels. For repairing sheet metal, welding in metal patch panels provides the best overall repair, but to do so requires a welder and patch panel, which are sometimes not available for the task at hand.

Fiberglass mat is commonly used when repairing holes or any time when a bulk buildup is required. It is made up of short strands of glass fibers that are bound together, but not woven. When the mat is saturated with fiberglass resin, it becomes quite pliable and easy to form into complex shapes. As each layer of fiberglass mat is added, the laminate becomes thicker and stiffer.

Fiberglass cloth is more suitable for repairing cracks, breaks, or holes where there are no or few complex shapes. Since fiberglass cloth is made up of glass thread that is woven together, it is difficult to mold to curved shapes without wrinkling. To get the cloth to lie flat when it must be used on a curved surface, you can make several small cuts in the cloth before applying the resin. Fiberglass cloth is thinner than fiberglass mat, so cloth should not be used when you are building up bulk in the repair area. However, a repair made with cloth will be stronger than an equal thickness repair made of mat since the cloth contains a higher percentage of glass.

Fiberglass mat and cloth are available in different widths, lengths, and weights for different size jobs. For the beginner, working with smaller pieces of cloth or mat will be easier than trying to work with larger pieces.

To bond fiberglass mat or cloth, you will need fiberglass resin. Resin is a two-part mixture comprising a thick liquid to which a much smaller amount per volume of hardener is added. The amount of hardener to use will vary depending on the ambient air temperature and humidity, as well as the amount of time you desire to work with the material. As the fiberglass resin cures or "kicks," a chemical reaction occurs between the liquid resin and the hardener.

As a result of this chemical reaction, two things happen: the fiberglass resin, mat, and cloth solidify, and they get very hot in the process. Due to this latter reason, adequate skin and eye protection is mandatory when working with fiberglass. Adequate ventilation is also a necessity as the odor of curing fiberglass is quite intense and can cause irritation for those with respiratory problems. After the fiberglass has cured, you should also wear a nuisance mask, eye protection, and skin covering any time that you are sanding, drilling, or cutting it.

To estimate how much resin you will need when making a repair, remember that each successive coat requires only half as much resin as the first coat. For the first coat, it will take approximately 1 pint of resin to thoroughly saturate 1 square yard of cloth, while $1\frac{1}{2}$ quarts of resin will be required to thoroughly saturate 1 square yard of mat.

When mixing and working with fiberglass, you should be thinking a "disposable" container rather than cleanable one. Fiberglass resin can be mixed in disposable paint tray liners, picnic/party cups, empty gallon milk jugs, or almost anything that is clean and will contain the liquid resin. Common paint stirrers work well to mix the resin and hardener, while disposable paintbrushes work well to spread the resin onto the cloth or mat. With all of the disposable containers available, replacing them is cheaper than the materials and time that would be required to clean them. Your hands, however, are not disposable, so you should cover them with latex gloves. You should also have some acetone available for cleanup should you happen to get some resin on your hands or skin.

Plastic Body Filler

No matter how good you may be with a body hammer, if you have straightened any sheet metal or installed any patch panels, you will probably need to apply at least a skim coat of body filler. True, there are some craftsmen who can metal finish a vehicle so perfectly that no filler is required, but you probably aren't at that point quite yet. Before applying any filler, you should take the time to consult with an expert to verify that you are using compatible materials. You will be much better off determining the appropriate filler product for your use before you use it, rather than being disappointed when a less than optimum product yields less than pleasing results. The main concern here is whether you are applying the body filler to sheet metal, galvanized steel, fiberglass, or aluminum. It is always better to do the work correctly the first time than to redo a lot of work or to be forced to live with less than desired results.

If you purchase your bodywork supplies from a dealer that sells these same materials to the professionals, you can rest assured that the person behind the counter knows which products are best for your particular application. However, if you purchase your body filler from the local discount department store, you may be hard pressed to find someone who even knows what the product is used for. You can be certain that most body fillers will say on the label that they are for use on bare metals, so unfortunately the info on the label does little to actually inform you of the appropriateness of the product on your particular project.

Plastic body fillers have evolved greatly since their inception as an alternative to lead. Several different companies now make plastic body filler, and most offer a variety of products to choose from, depending on your application. Some fillers are designed for use on fiberglass, while others are designed for use on sheet metal. Still others require an undercoat of epoxy primer to increase adhesion, and there are ones that should be applied directly to bare metal. Like various primer products, some fillers are for smoothing out rough bodywork, while others are used for finish coats. The point is that not all body fillers are created equal or even perform the same task. If you use the wrong type of filler, it will quickly reveal the location of any bodywork when the vehicle is parked in the sun. I doubt that you plan to keep your car parked in the garage forever.

BODY FILLERS

Product	Description	Characteristics	Typical Uses
Evercoat Everglass FIB-622	Short strand fiberglass reinforced body filler	High strength, high build, and waterproof	Repairing holes, rusted metal, body seams, and shattered fiberglass. Used as the first filler over any welds.
Evercoat Rage Gold FIB-112	Pinhole-free body filler	Superior adhesion to galvanized steel and aluminum; high-grade resin reduces risk of staining	Filling low areas of bodywork on galvanized steel or aluminum surfaces. Used as the second coat of filler over Everglass.
Evercoat Rage Xtreme FIB-120	Pinhole-free body filler	Self-leveling, easy spreading, easily sands with 80-grit sandpaper	Filling low areas of bodywork. Used to finish areas of Rage Gold.
Evercoat MetalWorks Z-Grip FIB-282	Lightweight body filler	Excellent adhesion to galvanized steel, aluminum, and epoxy primers	Filling corrosion prone areas.
Evercoat Metal Glaze FIB-416	Polyester finishing and blending putty	Can be used over bare metal and all body fillers	Used in conjunction with other Evercoat body fillers and glazing putties to enhance their ease of working.
Evercoat MetalWorks Spot-Lite FIB-445	Lightweight finishing putty	Excellent adhesion to galvanized steel, aluminum, and plastics	Final filling of galvanized steel, aluminum, and plastics.

Most likely, you will need at least a skim coat of body filler whenever you straighten sheet metal. Evercoat is one of several companies that manufacture a complete line of body fillers for various applications. The chart opposite will assist you in determining which filler is correct for your particular application.

The majority of body fillers are applied using the same methods, but you should read the directions for the particular product that you are using to be sure. Typically, the surface to be filled is sanded down to bare metal before filler is applied. Note that some fillers suggest that the surface be stripped of any paint and a coat of epoxy primer applied prior to use. Most auto body paint and supply stores will be able to provide printed information telling you specifically which products are and are not compatible.

Whether you are applying filler to bare metal (or fiberglass) or to a primered surface, some amount of filler material is spread onto a mixing board or mixing sheet, and then mixed *thoroughly* with a proportionate amount of hardener using a flexible spreader. The amount of hardener you should use will depend on your shop conditions, such as temperature and humidity. Practice is the best way to determine how much to use, but as a start, add a proportionate amount of hardener to the filler (i.e., a quarter

tube of hardener to a quarter of the container of filler). Too little hardener and it will not set up properly; too much hardener and it will set up right there on your mixing board. Yes, it will probably take the entire project before you get the proportionate amounts just right. If you do get it mixed a little too cool, you can speed the curing process slightly by placing a portable heater or heat lamp nearby. If the filler begins to "kick" before you have it spread out, you might as well scrape it off the mixing board and throw it away, as you won't be able to spread it properly.

Most body fillers use a hardener that is a distinctly different color than the filler itself. This makes it easy to tell when the two are mixed thoroughly, which is when the mix is the same color throughout. If there are streaks of color, you need to keep on mixing. When you have the filler and the hardener mixed thoroughly, scoop some filler onto a flexible spreader and spread it onto the area to be filled. Then make a couple of light passes over the area with an empty spreader to even out the filler.

For best results, don't apply body filler more than $1/8$ inch thick in total. If more than this is required, you should try to metal work the area being repaired slightly more before applying any filler. If it just isn't feasible to carry out any hammer and dolly work and the area to be filled is deeper than $1/8$ inch, fill it with two applications of filler, rather than attempting to fill it all at one time. Filler, like most auto body repair products, cures as its various chemical components react and escape from the material that is left. If the filler is applied too thick, it will quite often cure on the outside before all of the chemical reaction has taken place on the inside, trapping uncured material inside of the repair. When this happens, the repair won't last as long as it should and will ultimately show up in the finished paint job.

Some older types of filler require initial smoothing with a cheese grater–type file, while newer products can be smoothed initially with 80-grit sandpaper, but you should check with the person behind the shop counter to determine the best method. If you are using any type of filler that requires using a cheese grater, you will soon realize that the initial smoothing should be done slightly before the filler cures completely. You can watch the edges of the filler to get a feel for whether it has cured enough or not. If the filler starts breaking away at the edges or if the sandpaper starts loading up, the filler has not cured sufficiently. It is difficult to describe the correct time, but with a little bit of practice, you can quickly get a feel for it.

You want to knock off the high spots before the filler gets rock hard, but not too soon or you will easily gouge out more material than desired. As you begin working the filler, sand the entire filled area first with 80- or 100-grit sandpaper, then switch to 200- or 240-grit to blend the filler into the surrounding area. When you are finished, you will have a good idea if more filler is necessary or not prior to applying primer.

When you have finished sanding, blow all of the sanding dust away with an air nozzle. If there are low spots remaining, lightly rough up the area to be filled with the previously used grit of sandpaper, and then mix an appropriate amount of body filler and apply it as before. Work the second and successive layers of filler (if required) just as the first until any and all low areas are filled.

Sandpaper

Prior to applying sealer and paint, you will get plenty of opportunities to work with sandpaper, so there is no need to start using it too soon. Damaged body panels should be *straightened* long before any sanding is done. Sandpaper should be used for smoothing thin coats of body filler, scuffing a primed surface prior to application of additional coats of primer or sealer, and for wet sanding clear coats after the paint has been applied.

Although you may have heard of wet sanding, you may not know what it actually means or when it should be done. First of all, you must use sandpaper that is designed for, and labeled as, wet use, because if is not designed to be used wet, it will simply fall apart.

Wet sanding is typically done only after the vehicle has been painted. Extremely fine (1000-grit or finer) sandpaper should be moved in a circular motion with light pressure after being dipped in a water bucket or a surface that has been sprayed with water. The wet-sanding process removes the orange-peel effect from the paint, while the water helps to float away the paint that is being removed, rather than simply rubbing it back into the surface.

On some high-dollar, custom-built vehicles, the body person may use the wet-sanding technique prior to paint in order to get the smoothest surface possible. For repairs to your daily driver, this is probably overkill. It is also not a good idea to pour water on a piece of bare sheet metal or into an area of body filler. Unless you are a highly skilled body person, you don't need to be creating any more problems for yourself.

So, now that you know that most of your sanding is going to be done dry, grab yourself a dust mask and a sanding block. For removing paint and getting down to bare metal, a 36- or 50-grit disc on an electric or pneumatic sander works best if you are working on a localized repair. Entire panels that require complete paint removal should be

chemically stripped or media blasted. For initial shaping of body filler, use 80- or 100-grit sandpaper over the entire filled area and then switch to 200- or 240-grit sandpaper to blend the filler into the surrounding areas. The entire area that will require repainting after repair should then be sanded with 400-grit sandpaper.

Seam Sealer

Seam sealer is much like caulking for automobiles. Although it is available in forms that can be brushed on, it is typically dispensed from a tube. As its name implies, it is used to seal seams in sheet metal from moisture or dirt that would eventually allow rust to begin forming. Common areas of use include floor panels and in trunk areas where the floor meets the inner fender or wheelhouse. Any location that is prone to collecting and trapping moisture is a good candidate for seam sealer, as its application is much easier and less expensive than replacing rusty sheet metal. Most seam sealer products can be applied directly to bare sheet metal or over primered surfaces, but are usually applied prior to paint.

SPRAY APPLICATIONS

Bodywork itself doesn't require anything to be applied by spray, which means that you don't have to have an air compressor to straighten your recently dented fender. So, if you live in the desert where there is virtually no humidity and you are good enough with a hammer and dolly, you can metal finish your ride and be done. Oh, you aren't a metal smith and you are more than familiar with snow, salt, and rain? In that case, you need to work toward repainting the repaired area.

You will need access to an air compressor (or beg, pay, or coerce someone else) to apply the various substrates that fall between straightening and painting. Substrates are the assorted fillers and primers that are applied to the surface material prior to actually applying paint. These layers have just as much impact on the quality of the final paint job as the paint itself.

Etching or Epoxy Primer

If after doing the required bodywork, you were simply to apply paint without any primer, the paint would most likely begin peeling off quickly in large sections. Many American automobiles that were manufactured in the late 1980s and early 1990s commonly had this problem. Although these particular vehicles did have primer applied prior to painting, the primer was not compatible with the surface to be painted. The result was lots of vehicles with

PPG's DP-series of epoxy primer is an excellent self-etching primer that can be used directly on bare metal to provide corrosion protection. It also increases the adhesion qualities of body fillers and other primers. As a two-part epoxy, it comprises the actual primer and a hardener that must be mixed according to a specific mixing ratio prior to use. It can also be mixed in a different yet specific ratio for use as a sealer prior to color coats.

paint peeling off in sheets, leaving the surface below exposed to the weather.

Primer's main purpose is to promote adhesion between the surface being repaired and the subsequent topcoats, whether it is body filler or paint. No one universal primer product will adequately prepare every surface for paint. Primer must be chosen for the material that it is intended to cover. Fiberglass requires different primer than aluminum, which in turn requires different primer than galvanized steel. Some materials can be primed with regular primer, while others are better suited for epoxy primer.

Two main reasons for using epoxy primer are its superior corrosion protection and its excellent adhesion qualities, yet epoxy primer cannot be used for every application. You should consult with your local paint jobber store for its recommendations on the best primer for your particular needs. Any time a sheet-metal panel is stripped (chemically or mechanically) to bare metal, it should be cleaned and coated with etching or epoxy primer as soon as practical to avoid the formation of surface rust. Most body fillers can be applied over etching or epoxy primer, so there will be no reason to go back to bare metal during the repair process.

Polyester Spray Body Filler

A relatively new primer product is sprayable body filler, which can be used over bare metal, aluminum, fiberglass, and most other body fillers. Since this is a thicker filler-type material than most primers or paints, it will require using a spray-gun nozzle tip of 2.2 millimeters or larger. You should apply three or four light coats, and then block sand with 120-grit sandpaper. Then apply a guide coat (dusting) of a contrasting color spray enamel. This guide coat should then be block sanded with 180-grit sandpaper, another guide coat applied, and then block sanded with 220-grit sandpaper.

Primer-Surfacer

Having a high solids content, primer-surfacers (also known as high build primer) are used to cover slight imperfections such as sanding scratches. These products should not be confused with, or used as, fillers, as they are not intended to fill more than slight scratches. Primer-surfacers are the last of the undercoat products that are designed to be sanded smooth.

After applying primer-surfacer, you should block sand it smooth with 320-grit sandpaper. Then apply a second coat, allow it to dry, and apply a guide coat of a contrasting color of spray can enamel. Block sand the guide coat with 400-grit paper, and then with 500-grit until you have removed all of the guide coat.

Sealers

To prevent the solvent from topcoats seeping into the various undercoats, a sealer should be applied. This will add maximum adhesion capabilities and ensure uniform color match. Sealers should also be used whenever applying new paint over a factory finish that has been baked on at temperatures around 450 degrees Fahrenheit. With the durability and hardness of these factory finishes, it is difficult for new paint to penetrate the surface and establish proper adhesion. If new paint is applied without first scuffing (using 180- to 220-grit sandpaper) and sealing the surface, then the new paint will most likely flake off or even peel off in sheets.

MASKING SUPPLIES

Although HVLP spray guns minimize the amount of primer or paint overspray, you still need to mask off areas where you don't want whatever you may be spraying. Even though proper masking takes a fair amount of time, it takes less time than cleaning overspray from unwanted areas.

Omni is a budget-minded series of paint and refinish products made by PPG. Shown is its primer-surfacer that is used to fill sanding scratches in sheet metal or body filler. Known as a high fill primer, still it does not take the place of body filler. A high percentage of primer-surfacer is sanded off in the block sanding process of perfecting the body prior to paint application.

Masking Tape

Everyone is familiar with ordinary hardware or household grade masking tape; however, it should not be used when spraying automotive primers and paint products. Ordinary household masking tape has not been treated to withstand the potent solvents that are used in automotive paint. Additionally, adhesives used in ordinary masking tape are not designed to break loose easily from surfaces and therefore can remain on painted bodies after the bulk of material has been pulled off. The lingering residue might require use of a mild solvent for complete removal, a chore that could threaten the finish or new paint applied next to it. Whether your project consists of a very small paint touchup or complete paint job, you have to realize that automotive paint masking tape is the only product designed for such use. Using any other type of inexpensive alternative is just asking for problems and aggravation.

Automotive grade masking tape is available in sizes ranging from $\frac{1}{8}$ inch up to 2 inches wide. You will likely need $\frac{3}{4}$-inch masking tape for most purposes, but having a couple of extra sizes will make your masking work easier. It is much simpler to place a few strips of 2-inch-wide masking tape over a headlight, than to maneuver a sheet of masking paper over that relatively small area.

Masking Paper

Rolls of quality automotive paint masking paper are available at auto body paint supply stores in widths ranging from 4 inches up to 3 feet. Masking paper is chemically treated to prevent paint or solvent from penetrating it. Seldom will you find professional auto painters using anything but treated masking paper for any masking job. Although newspaper material may seem inexpensive and appropriate for paint masking chores, it is porous and can let paint seep through to mar surface finishes underneath. Everyone who uses masking paper will tell you that a masking paper dispenser is worth the extra money, as it makes masking the vehicle much easier and faster.

Fine Line Tape

For masking along trim or moldings that cannot be removed prior to priming or painting, use $\frac{1}{8}$-inch 3M Fine Line tape. It is easy to use as a primary masking edge along trim and molding edges, as it is very maneuverable, and will adhere securely around curves without bending or folding. After placing the Fine Line tape at the edge of whatever is being masked, $\frac{3}{4}$-inch masking tape can be attached to the Fine Line tape without the need to be right at the edge of the masked area.

CHAPTER 3
DEVELOPING A REPAIR STRATEGY

Okay, it actually happened. You, your spouse, son, or daughter got into a minor fender bender. The damage doesn't look too extensive. For reasons that have already been discussed, you don't want to turn it in to your insurance, but don't want to pay what the body shop quote says it cost. Now is the time to step up to the plate and fix it yourself. However, before you pick up a hammer and dolly, you need to assess the damage and develop a repair strategy. Having a plan will play a major part toward getting the vehicle repaired and back on the road in a timely manner.

ASSESSING THE DAMAGE

There may be some portions of the damaged vehicle that can be repaired and some that are beyond repair. At this point you need to determine which ones are which—what can you fix, and what must you replace?

Unless you are sure that the damage is limited to exterior sheet metal, you might want to take the damaged vehicle to a reputable body shop for an estimate, if you have not done so already. This will serve you in a couple of ways, and possibly more if you are completely new to auto

A dented plastic bumper/fascia assembly like this is typically replaced by an auto repair shop if the insurance company is paying for the repair. If you are tackling the work yourself, however, you can repair this. By using a heat gun (something more substantial than a hair dryer), you can heat the panel until it becomes pliable and then push it out close to its original shape. You can then leave as is for a no-cost repair, or apply a skim coat of filler, sand, and repaint.

Severe damage to a passenger car's rear quarter panel is often the cause of a total loss of the vehicle. If the vehicle is not totaled, the repair often consists of cutting out the affected panel and welding in a replacement. On this Ford Explorer, however, damage was minimal, requiring only some minor bodywork, priming, and block sanding. The affected area was masked off and repainted later in the day.

repair and will need to purchase tools to make the repair. First, and most importantly, an experienced service writer will know what to look for as far as hidden damage and will often list the parts that need to be replaced. This will give you a better idea of what you are getting yourself into. Secondly, the quote will of course tell you how much the body shop will charge to complete the repair. If the repair is very labor intensive, you will quickly realize that your labor rate is much more affordable than the shop's is, providing you have the time. If a hammer and dolly, a gallon of plastic body filler, some sandpaper, and a quart of paint will be your only expenses, you can do the work for less money than what you would pay the body shop. Additionally, if you have been wanting to purchase an air compressor or other tools anyway, using them for this repair might make buying them more justifiable. They are expensive, but if you can get the tools you want and get the car fixed for the same money . . . I can give you the idea, but you still have to sell the idea to the holder of the purse strings.

If you take your damaged vehicle to an auto body repair shop, a very common question from the service writer will be: "Is your insurance paying for this or are you?" Your answer doesn't mean that the service writer will automatically jack up the price if the insurance company is paying for it, but it will have an impact on how the repair is made, and therefore the bottom line. Since insurance companies are also usually paying for loaner cars while yours is being repaired, they want your vehicle back to you as soon as possible. What this all boils down to is that many sheet-metal panels that could be repaired by a competent body man are replaced in the interest of time. These replacement parts are more expensive to purchase, but they require less labor to refinish. Depending on the particular vehicle, the parts may be much more expensive than the necessary labor. Additionally, there is disassembly and reassembly labor to be factored into the quote. It is quite conceivable that two quotes for the same damaged vehicle (one to replace, one to repair) could be substantially different.

What Can Be Repaired?

Of course, we know that you are going to take on this repair yourself and all of the money spent on it is coming straight out of your pocket. Since your labor rate is negligible at this point, you should straighten, smooth, and refinish every damaged piece that you can, rather than replace it.

In body shops that do insurance work, many brackets, actuator levers, and other hidden parts that are damaged slightly are replaced rather than repaired. The logic is that the customer turns the repair over to their insurance company so that they will be made correctly and completely. That's why we all pay for insurance, so that when something bad does happen, the bad goes away, and it's as if nothing had happened.

However, some of these brackets could be straightened if desired. You are not going to see these particular parts that are inside the hood, door, or deck lid anyway, so you shouldn't care if some paint is chipped a little. And, as long as the piece functions properly, you can live with it, right? That's where you have to decide what can be repaired. A reputable body shop will err toward customer satisfaction because its reputation is at stake. When you are repairing your own vehicle, it is your wallet that is most vulnerable.

Note that some things can be repaired that should not be. Perhaps you've had the experience of driving behind a car that seems to be going down the road off-kilter—you can see all four tires even though it's driving straight. That vehicle has suffered structural damage and been returned, imprudently, to the road. If your car has been impaired in its drivability—e.g., it doesn't steer right or shift right or there is a braking problem—do not plunge forward with a welder, some donor parts, and a cavalier attitude. Have any structural or operational damage assessed by an automotive repair professional. You don't want something that looks OK but will not operate safely—one wreck is enough.

This pickup truck tailgate was damaged quite a bit, so it was replaced rather than repaired. Since this repair was being covered by the owner's insurance, the latch mechanism, linkage, and brackets were also replaced to make sure that the tailgate will operate correctly. If you were making the repair yourself, you could save some money by spending a little bit of time straightening these components.

The old latch mechanism is to the left and the replacement to the right. If you look closely, you will see that the brass colored rod is bent slightly on the original latch. Using this damaged latch could make it difficult to open the tailgate. The linkage rods and brackets, however, could be straightened with little or no adverse effects. None of the damaged components will be seen when reinstalled, except for the outer portion of the latch, which is not damaged.

What Must Be Replaced?

Given enough time, almost any dented automotive sheet metal can be straightened. However, if any of those panels have a crease pressed into them as the result of an accident, you should probably consider replacing the affected panel, as the crease would be very difficult to remove. If there are small rips or tears in sheet-metal panels, they can be repaired by welding the metal back together, even if it requires welding in a patch panel.

Many newer vehicles have plastic panels around the traditional bumper areas at the front or rear of the vehicle. Some of these panels are made of rigid plastic that will break upon impact. Provided that the pieces are all there and can be clamped back together in the correct shape, they can be repaired. If significant portions of the panel are missing, or are damaged to the point that there is no way to clamp them back into the correct shape, you may be time ahead to simply purchase a replacement part. Other plastic panels are made to be more flexible and are less likely to break. However, this softer plastic will distort if pushed beyond its resilient state. If it undergoes a simple dent that is created by a single point of contact, it is possible to repair the dent, while multiple forces from different directions will most likely distort the panel beyond reasonable repair.

While some pieces are available from dealers or as reproductions in the aftermarket, remember the auto salvage industry. You can save a considerable amount of money buying a used, but otherwise whole and functional, part from a salvage yard over what you'd pay from the Internet or a dealer's parts counter. Whenever possible, bring the old part with you for comparison. Of course another option is looking on websites like www.car-part.com, which allow you to search for almost anything you would need.

Analysis of Repair versus Replacement

Determining which parts are unsalvageable and which can be fixed is not necessarily the end of your inquiry. We all have demands on our time, so practicality is always a consideration. Once you've decided which parts can be fixed, make your best estimate as to the amount of time said repair will take. Can the repairs be broken down into smaller steps so that one or two steps toward the complete repair can be made on a weekend? Even if it takes a month of weekends to finish the repair, you can save yourself some labor fees. If you can't actually repair the affected panels in this timeframe, can you replace the damaged parts and get them primed and painted within your time constraints? For example, if a door got hit and this broke the window, you'd have to disassemble the door, remove the broken glass, most likely repair the window track, get replacement glass, etc., before you fix the dent. That's a lot of work—doable but time consuming. You're better off buying a good door from a wrecking yard and putting your effort into cosmetics.

Especially as an amateur, you will find that project phases take longer than you anticipate. Replacing the door as discussed requires driving to a salvage yard, getting the replacement, removing the old one and fitting the new. Repainting it, unless you're so lucky that it matches your vehicle's paint already, will add to your time. Do you need to install the replacement for interim driving, and remove it again later for the paint work, or can you leave it off and

handle that now, saving the on-and-off time? Of course you could paint it on the vehicle, too, but you'll spare yourself masking time and effort if you spray it separate.

External deadlines may also come into play—like a child needing to drive the vehicle to college. Here's an idea: get that family member involved in the repair work. This will help him or her learn to appreciate the consequences of an accident, and may also empower him or her to take on repair and maintenance tasks in the future. A little self-sufficiency is good for all of us and a good parent-child project can turn a chore into quality family time.

MATERIALS

If you are not tied to a deadline or otherwise constricted by time, you can purchase the required body hammers, dollies, and body filler for less than the price of a replacement fender. If there are multiple panels that require repair

Besides the drivetrain components that suffered considerable damage, the front fender, bumper/fascia assembly, and headlight all required replacement on this Buick. A portion of the fender was actually torn away and the plastic bumper/fascia assembly was distorted beyond its resilient state, making replacement rather than repair a must. The time spent trying to repair this damage would simply exceed the cost of panel replacement.

or replacement, the cash investment in tools spreads itself out over the entire repair. Additionally, when the repair is complete, you will have more tools in your tool box and the experience to use them, so you will be better off in that way. At least you will be better equipped to handle the situation should it occur again—definitely something to consider if this repair has occurred because of your oldest offspring and you have others who will learn to drive in the future. Even if it isn't their fault, young drivers will typically be involved in more automobile accidents—just ask your auto insurance broker.

OVERALL REFINISH QUALITY

Okay, are you repairing the vehicle that your teenage son or daughter is still using to learn how to drive or is it the one that your spouse drives? If the repair to be completed has you wondering if you are capable, you should ask yourself "how good does it have to be?" If you purchased a relatively cheap vehicle that already has more than a few minor dents and dings for your teenager to drive, the repair doesn't have to be on par with what would be required on a brand-new vehicle. Yes, you still want to fix it and look decent, but you should probably lean toward repairing rather than replacing panels in this situation.

On the other hand, if the vehicle is in pretty good condition other than your recently acquired smashed fender, replacing said fender or other panels could save you some time. That time could then be spent on high quality detailing, which will go a long way toward making the vehicle look like new again.

DETERMINING THE REQUIRED PARTS

Whether the recently damaged vehicle is being repaired at a professional collision repair shop or by you in your garage (or even driveway), the repair process starts with an estimate. This is when the body shop estimator and the insurance adjuster make it or break it for their respective employers. Their task is to thoroughly inspect the damaged vehicle to determine which parts must be replaced versus which parts can be repaired. While they are doing this, they are compiling a complete list of parts that will need to be replaced, repaired, or refinished. The more thorough the list, the more accurate the estimate will be.

To complete the repair in a timely and efficient manner, you will need to do an estimate as well. Grab a clipboard with a pad of paper and a pen, as you will not be able to remember everything. Professional estimators have experience in knowing how vehicles come apart and go back together. You may not have that knowledge, but you can take the time to pull damaged items and look for other parts in need of attention.

Although disassembly may reveal additional damage and expand your list, begin collecting all of the parts that you think you will need as soon as it's practical to do so. Some items, like a fender or hood, you may need to acquire just before you start work in the interests of space, but gather everything for which you have room. You don't want to set aside a weekend, get part way into the repair and then have to stop working because you're missing a critical piece.

New Parts

Different sources for replacement panels are available with pricing and quality being the significant differences. New parts usually come from one of two sources: the original manufacturer (or licensed parts supplier), or a manufacturer of reproduction parts. Parts from the original manufacturer may be identified as original equipment manufacturer (OEM) or new old stock (NOS)—which describes OEM parts that are no longer "new" in terms of time, but are new because they have never been used before. For older vehicles, especially collector cars, NOS parts can command high prices. Reproduction parts can be built by anyone, so the buyer should beware as quality varies from one manufacturer to another. This quality goes not just for metal thickness but also for the accuracy of the reproduction. Cheap panels may not align properly with mounting holes and contours and may require additional work to make them fit. In some cases, as when the damage is rust along a lower portion, you may be better off cutting out the damaged area and welding in a patch panel than trying to achieve the same fit with an entire replacement panel.

Genuine replacement panels from your vehicle's manufacturer are what would be used by your vehicle dealer's body shop if it was hired to make the repair. These replacement panels are brand-new sheet metal, with the original mounting holes, light recesses, and contours. As you might expect, these are the most expensive to purchase, although their higher quality fit will save time and trouble. They also typically come in primer, saving some prep time.

OEM or NOS

These new parts are usually as close as your local new-car dealership parts department. If what you seek is not in stock, you will need to check for estimated delivery time. In addition to having the right parts, the guys and gals at the parts counter have access to lots of assembly drawings, which might be helpful to you. Depending on the person

When shopping for replacement panels, you will need to verify exactly how much metal you must replace prior to buying, as several similar panels may be available. Do you need a panel that replaces only the wheel opening contours, all the way up to the top ridge of the rear quarter, or all the way to the trunk opening?

behind the counter, he or she may or may not be willing to print you a copy, but he or she will usually allow you to take a look at the drawings. This will give you some insight to any additional parts that you may need to replace.

An advantage of buying from an automotive dealer is that most parts that have not been modified can be returned if you realize that you do not actually need them. Hang onto your receipt and the packaging for possible returns. You may be required to pay a restocking fee, but that is considerably less than being stuck with the unnecessary part. Additionally, dealerships will usually accept cash, check, or credit cards, the latter sometimes being an evil necessity in the case of an automobile accident.

Reproduction

Reproduction parts are only as good as the aftermarket manufacturer desires to make them, as there is no governing body that regulates their manufacture. There are several companies that manufacture very good replacement parts, while there are others that leave plenty to be desired. Any problems with proper fit are usually not noticeable until after you have purchased the part, tried to install it, and found out that it does not fit. On the other hand, some of these replacement panels are superior. It pays to ask around before you buy. The cost of the part is not always a good indication of the quality either, so do some research before you plunk down your money. Reproduction parts that are approved or officially licensed by the OEM will be marked accordingly. For example, Goodmark Industries' parts are approved by Chrysler and labeled with Mopar Authentic Restoration Product logos. General Motors and Ford have similar labels for parts made by aftermarket sources that meet their approval.

Sheetmetal parts from some reproduction companies are not primed, and therefore may have some surface rust that must be removed prior to installation. It is sometimes

This particular full quarter covers all of the side and also wraps over to the edge of the trunk opening and the bottom of the sail panel, making for a pretty complete rear quarter repair on this early Mustang.

necessary to elongate mounting holes in order to get panels to align properly. Also, some of these panels are somewhat wavy, requiring additional block sanding prior to painting.

Used Parts

For everyday vehicles, like Toyota Corollas and Ford Explorers, the average salvage yard is likely to have what you need at a fraction of a new part's cost. Because it's their business, most salvage yards know what range of years a given fender or hood or door will fit, but you should also investigate this information on your own, to spare yourself a return trip. Parts may vary by model and specification too, so bring as much information as possible to the yard or explain it in your phone conversation. If it's feasible, bring the part you need to replace to the yard so you can do a part-to-part comparison before you buy.

Another alternative to new parts is reconditioned components. Parts available in this condition that may need replacement following an accident include starters, alternators, radiators, fuel tanks, etc. A properly reconditioned component will usually come with some sort of warranty and should function as good as new.

DETERMINING THE REQUIRED LABOR

This book is in your hands because you've decided to tackle the repair yourself. But it needn't be only you. Generally, everything you can do adequately, you will not have to pay someone else to tackle, yet some things you may want to turn over to a pro. It depends on how much time you have available and your comfort level. A windshield is an unwieldy and fragile part that many people don't want to replace at home. Maybe the radiator is damaged and you want your mechanic to fix that and make sure everything runs OK before you tackle the body and paint. Perhaps this isn't a collision we're talking about but some rust you want to get rid of. You may be ready to learn painting but aren't prepared to cut and weld patch panels.

As you assess what it will take in time and dollars to fix the damage, note too which tasks you will tackle or seek professional assistance. For every task you won't handle, find the pro and get both a ballpark price and a timeframe within which the shop can do the work. You will need to factor in these considerations to get all necessary repairs done.

Chassis or Unibody Straightening

If the chassis or unibody shell is bent, the only way to correct it is to have it straightened on a frame straightening table—if it is not beyond repair. Most professional auto body repair shops have the equipment to do this or can recommend a shop that does.

The basic process for straightening is to drive (or winch) the vehicle onto the rack, take measurements at specific locations with precise measuring equipment, and then pull the chassis or unibody back into correct alignment by using hydraulic jacks that are part of the frame straightening table. This frame straightening process squares up the chassis and should not be confused with a wheel alignment, which aligns the wheels to the chassis.

Mechanical Repair

Besides the body panels being damaged in an automobile accident, it is quite possible that mechanical items will need repair or replacement as well. Some of these items are typically completed by the auto body repair shop, while other repairs will require work to be completed by a mechanic. It is common for the auto body shop to install a new radiator, recharge an air conditioning system, or various other tasks that only require bolting on a new part.

Since the vehicle being repaired is yours, there is nothing saying that you cannot make all of the repairs. This simply depends on your automotive knowledge and experience, your tool and equipment availability, and your willingness and ability to learn new tasks. However, if you do not possess everything that is required to repair the vehicle to the point of being safe and reliable, send that portion of the repair to a professional.

Glass Replacement

Besides sheet metal and radiators, the other most vulnerable component in an automobile accident is the window glass. If any of it is cracked or broken, it should be replaced, and it must be replaced if it impedes the driver's field of vision through the front windshield. Replacement glass can be purchased through your local automotive glass shop. You can consult your local telephone listing to quickly find an automotive glass shop in your area.

Installing glass is not as difficult as you might believe, but since the material is fragile, making a mistake could cost you more money than you save by doing it yourself. Incorrect installation could get the glass in a bind, which would make it susceptible to cracking or breaking, and improper sealing could cause leaks. Depending on your skills and comfort level, glass installation is one part of the repair that you may want to subcontract. For more on glass replacement, see Chapter 6.

CHAPTER 4
DISASSEMBLY AND STRIPPING

Most auto body repairs, whether prompted by a collision or a restoration effort, will require a certain amount of disassembly. Whether the parts removed will be replaced or repaired and refinished, or come off merely to allow access to other parts, methodical disassembly is a must.

Some sheet-metal parts will require you to strip off previous finishes in order to obtain the best possible results with the new applications of body filler or paint. This removal of paint or rust can be done by media blasting, chemical dipping, or by grinding and sanding.

DISASSEMBLY

Rather than simply unbolting everything haphazardly, not paying attention to what kinds of fasteners are used, and in general causing more trouble for yourself later on in the reassembly process, you should take your time and think about what you are doing. Develop some method of organization and storage, so that reassembly will go smoothly and therefore be a more enjoyable process that is more likely to prevent the need for additional repair or paint touchup.

Fasteners

OEMs use standard, metric, and specialty fasteners to assemble the vehicles that we drive. None of them are any better than others, but they do require the proper set of tools to be able to work with them efficiently. Older American-built vehicles (1970 and older) will almost exclusively have standard fasteners. Newer American-built vehicles will most likely have some standard, metric, or specialty fasteners, while imported vehicles will most likely be limited to metric and specialty fasteners. Of course, any vehicle is subject to non-stock fasteners having been installed by a previous owner or technician who has done work on the vehicle.

For most auto body disassembly, a set of $^3/_8$-inch drive sockets and combination wrenches in standard and metric sizes (as required) will suffice for most of the fasteners. A set of $^1/_4$-inch drive sockets will overlap fasteners that can be removed with the $^3/_8$-inch drive set, but will be easier to use in some instances where accessibility is limited. You

may also need socket extensions of various lengths. You most likely will not need 1-inch drive sockets unless you are working on heavy-duty trucks, or are removing rusty bumper bolts from an older vehicle that actually has a real bumper. Rust or other corrosion, or even some impact damage, may make these larger bolts a little more difficult to remove than their smaller counterparts. Some bolts may require a breaker bar to increase your leverage, or an impact wrench. Any type of chisel (air chisel or hammer and chisel) should be reserved as a last resort for disassembly, as this method will most likely destroy the bolts. If you have exhausted all other methods, an air chisel will greatly speed the disassembly process and make you want to pound your chest when you are done. Of course, you'll need to acquire replacement fasteners for any you destroy prior to the reassembly process.

A pneumatic ratchet will save lots of wrist and elbow fatigue if you have several fasteners to remove. It also works great when removing and reinstalling fasteners, as long as a great deal of torque is not required.

Should certain screws present something other than slotted or Phillips heads—such as Torx, Allen head, or clutch head—don't try to loosen them until you find or buy a tool that fits correctly. Torx screws and clutch head screws have a specific shape other than a slot in the head, and Allen head bolts have a hex shape recessed into the bolt head, requiring the proper-sized Allen wrench for removal and installation.

Still other specialty plastic fasteners are removed by slipping a specific type of pliers beneath their heads from each side and then prying them loose. Due to their typically larger head, these fasteners are very common on late model vehicles and are used to attach many of the flexible fascias and inner fender panels where a typical bolt could cause stress cracks in the fascia or pull through the more flexible inner fender panels.

Typical Methods of Attachment

Knowing how various components are attached to your vehicle will no doubt make their disassembly or removal

In this photo, both of the front fenders, as well as the grille, bumper, headlights, and all related front-end components have been removed. Whether they are being replaced or repaired, you can bet that each piece will be retained until the entire vehicle is refinished and reassembled to verify that all nuts, bolts, and emblems are reinstalled.

much easier. Although it would be nearly impossible to list methods of attachment for every vehicle, the following should provide a decent guide. Before jumping into a part removal procedure with both feet, carefully inspect each item to determine just how it is mounted. Unnecessary prying force breaks parts, an inconvenience that also costs money for replacement.

Exterior door handles and mirrors are typically secured with screws, nuts, or bolts. Some door handles are secured by a relatively large screw in line with the door handle and are located on the door edge. After removing the screw, you can pull out the handle from the door skin so that you can dislodge the linkage arms. Other door handles are usually secured by two smaller screws or nuts accessed from inside the inner door space. This requires removal of the interior door panel.

Interior door panels are usually secured by either screws or clips. You will have to examine the door panels on your car to determine how they are attached. If no screws are visible around the perimeter of the panel, chances are good that it features plastic clips pushed into retainer mounts. You can simply pry them loose; however, be sure to remove armrests, window cranks, and door handles beforehand.

Armrests are commonly secured by one or two large head screws. Window cranks on older cars are secured in place with a small C-shaped metal clip that must be pried off the crank's operating shaft for removal. Newer cars with window cranks may have pop-off plastic caps hiding the fastener. Use a small-bladed screwdriver to gently pry off the cap to access screws or nuts that hold the crank in place. Power window or power door lock switches must be pushed inward through the panel that houses them due to their wiring housed in the door itself.

To remove the interior door handles on older cars, detach their C-shaped metal clips in similar fashion as their matching window cranks. Newer car handles will have one or two screws holding them in place. After removing the screws, you might have to gently pry on the handle housing to pop it loose from the door panel. You will also have to remove the linkage arms from the handle to the door latch mechanism.

Light assemblies are normally secured with screws located on the back side. Taillights can be removed from inside the trunk or hatchback area or pulled straight out from the outside after removing the mounting hardware. Some lights may require the lenses to be removed first by removing a number of Phillips or Torx head screws. You should be able to easily remove the reflectors by loosening screws located at either end of the lens or from inside the corresponding compartment.

On older vehicles that use a sealed beam headlight, you should leave the headlights in place if possible, especially if they are correctly adjusted. If the headlights must be removed, try to avoid touching the two screws that have springs beneath them. These are the directional adjustment screws used to move the headlight up, down, right, or left. Headlight assemblies on newer vehicles are essentially a clear box with a reflector, in which a headlight bulb can be inserted from behind. With this headlight design, headlight aiming is not as critical as with sealed beam headlights.

Emblems, badges, and trim on older cars were attached with studs that were inserted through holes in the sheet metal and secured with clips or threaded nuts. Although gaining access to the back side may be difficult, removal is straightforward once you reach the fastener and remove it. On newer vehicles, these emblems and insignia are attached with adhesive or double-backed tape. By using a heat gun, the emblem can usually be peeled away easily.

Newer Vehicles

Mounting bolt positions vary across makes and models, so it is impossible to give a completely accurate location; however, the following can be used as a general guide. On newer vehicles (those that have a wraparound fascia rather than a separate bumper), the front and rear fascia typically slides into grooves or tracks on the inner fender or body shell. It is then secured to the vehicle by screws or bolts through the end of the fascia panel into holes along the wheelwell. This design makes for easy alignment and allows the fasteners to be less noticeable,

as they are partially obscured by the wheel and tire, yet still easy enough to access.

Front fenders are typically secured to the inner fender by a series of bolts along the top edge, which are accessible by opening the hood. They usually have one or two bolts located low on the fender near the front of the door and possibly in front of the wheel as well, but this will vary largely based on panel design.

Doors, hoods, and deck lids can usually be unbolted from their hinges, although an inner panel may need to be removed to provide access. Unless the hinges have been damaged and require replacement, they should be left in place to aid in proper alignment upon reassembly.

Grilles and headlights will vary greatly in their attachment points, as they tend to have styling that wraps them more around the side of the fender. On some vehicles, the grille will need to be removed prior to removing the headlights, while other vehicles will require the opposite.

Older Vehicles

On older vehicles that have real bumpers, whose attaching bolt's head is not so offensive to a vehicle designer, panels are typically easier to remove simply for the reason that the bolts are easier to find. Bumpers typically attach to bumper brackets with between four and eight bolts, and the brackets are secured to the vehicle's chassis with four to eight bolts as well.

Front fenders attach to the inner fender with a series of bolts like newer vehicles, but there are typically more bolts securing the fender to the radiator coil support in front of the wheel opening and to the body shell behind the wheel opening.

Hoods are normally attached to a spring/hinge assembly, rather than a simple hinge. For ease of reassembly, leave the spring/hinge assembly where it is unless it must be replaced. If it must be removed, use some masking tape on the panel that it mounts to as an aid in correct placement when reinstalling. Doors and deck lids can usually be removed from their hinges by removing two or three bolts from each hinge.

Grilles, headlights, and taillights are designed to flow with the fenders and hood, but are typically attached more independently. Grilles and headlights are usually attached to the radiator's core support, while the taillights generally mount directly to the vehicle's rear quarter panel or tail panel.

Documentation

Anything that can assist you in properly disassembling your vehicle is of great benefit. Although there are

REMOVING A FRONT BUMPER/FASCIA ASSEMBLY

Late model vehicles no longer have bumpers that are a separate, chrome-plated piece of steel as they once were a couple of decades ago. Back then, a big sturdy bumper was designed to ward off oncoming traffic with its brute strength. That theory for passenger protection has changed over the years, with the result being that most passenger cars and light-duty pickup trucks have a flexible bumper/fascia assembly.

This flexible assembly diffuses the impact force and minimizes the amount of potentially deadly force that reaches the passenger compartment. In a low impact situation, the bumper/fascia will flex, sustaining only scratches and marred paint. In a more significant impact, the bumper/fascia will most likely break and/or dent, but will diffuse energy in the process.

If you are working on a vehicle that has this type of bumper/fascia assembly (front or rear), you will need to know how to remove it, whether it is to repair or replace it. All vehicles will be slightly different in their attachment, but they will be similar to this example.

Left: Many of today's passenger vehicles use reusable plastic fasteners to attach various body panels. These fasteners work by being pushed into place and then expanding, much like a rivet. If you have a pair of pliers like the ones shown, which are designed especially for these fasteners, you can first squeeze the fastener and then pry it out, allowing you to reuse it. Without these pliers, you will probably have to destroy the fastener to remove it.

Below: This late model Buick has a flexible deflector that connects to the bumper/fascia in the front and sides. To remove the bumper/fascia assembly, this deflector will need to be removed as well. Most fasteners will be some type of self-tapping fastener.

After removing all of the bolts from the deflector, the bumper/fascia assembly is typically still secured by fasteners into the front fenders. With those bolts removed, the bumper/fascia assembly can be slid forward and removed. Since the material is much lighter than sheet-metal assemblies, it usually requires just one person to remove it.

After the bumper/fascia assembly is removed, additional damaged pieces can be removed. Using a pneumatic ratchet will speed the process, but is not a requirement. Disassembly is simply a matter of looking for, and removing all of, the fasteners that appear to be holding the particular piece in place. If it still does not come off, keep looking, just as professional body workers are required to do.

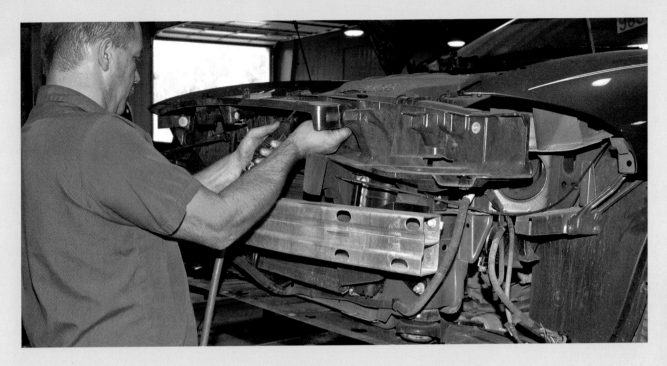

In this particular case, the hood release cable has to be disconnected from the latch prior to removing the latch assembly.

A poor design in the eyes of the body worker is this hood release cable passing through a hole in the panel, shown at the top of the photo. To remove this panel, the release cable will need to be removed. Additionally, it most likely will need to be passed back through this same hole upon reassembly to reach its destination and operate correctly.

literally volumes of documents on disassembly/reassembly of engines, transmissions, and other mechanical aspects of the automobile, similar information for body components is relatively rare, even in commercial body shops. Guys and gals who work in auto body shops on a full-time basis learn the process of disassembly by experience. They find that doors typically attach to the body in the same way, regardless of make or model. They also learn that fender attachment is similar, but that GM will use a particular fastener, while Ford may use some different type of fastener. Since these professionals learn by experience, where do you go for assistance?

Repair Manual

Even though you may not be able to find an auto body repair reference for your specific vehicle, any repair manual for your specific vehicle, such as those by Chilton or Haynes, can provide some information. Even if there is no specific text that addresses panel removal, drawings or photos that show how various mechanical aspects may attach or otherwise interfere with panel removal will be beneficial. If you live in a metropolitan area, call your main library and ask what automotive resources it has. Some libraries have rather extensive automotive collections, including online databases with detailed exploded drawings.

Notes and Photos

OK, you may have to dive in and proceed with the disassembly process the same way the professionals do—with intuition and by trial and error. No matter how intuitive you are or how good your memory, do yourself a favor and make some documentation for yourself. Take some notes as to what size bolt (and perhaps more importantly, what size wrench) is required to attach the fender, for example. Write down how many bolts are used and what kind they are. Washers can be important here to prevent things from slipping apart, so note them too—where do they go and on which side of the given pieces.

Draw rough sketches in a notebook if you don't have a digital camera. If you do, set it for close-up photography and document how it looks before and as you remove parts. You will be amazed how all of the bolts securing a front clip suddenly look alike when they are all together in a coffee can or a jar. Also, make notes on whether all of the fasteners are similar, except for a few. Are two of the three screws securing a bracket a different length than the third? What is different about these fasteners and what else do they attach to that necessitates their difference? You will find that many fasteners are used to attach multiple components, so when you cannot remove a panel even though you have removed all of the bolts that seem obvious, a fastener may be securing something to the opposite side of the panel.

A combination of notes and photographs will be most helpful when it's time to put it all together. You should download the photos the same evening that you have taken them to a file with an appropriate name, like Bumper-Photos. If you just leave them on your camera "for later," you may have so many other photos on there when you go to put your car together that you'll give up and just wing it. In other words, you'll render the photographs and time it took to snap them worthless. If you're organized, you can have your laptop with your well-organized photo files on a clean shelf and use your own "digital manual" at reassembly time.

Storage

Storage of disassembled parts while you are making repairs to other parts will begin to take up considerable amounts of room. Unless you are extremely organized or have vast amounts of storage space available, these parts will seem to expand the longer that they are disconnected from the vehicle. The more you can do to keep the parts organized and available when you are ready for them, but out of the way until then, the better off you will be.

However, don't be too quick to dispose of items, even if you think they are going to be replaced. Often times, a necessary mounting bolt, gasket, or other seemingly insignificant part will not be included with the replacement. Even if you are not required to scavenge from these old parts, they often serve as an invaluable reminder of how the particular assembly is to be reinstalled or connected. So, do not dispose of any parts until the repair is completely finished and the vehicle is back on the road.

Small Parts

Relatively small parts, such as door handles, mirrors, headlight assemblies, taillight assemblies, and their respective mounting hardware need to be kept together as separate units whenever possible. Any of these parts that are replacements should be kept in the box until they are attached to the vehicle for the last time. For parts that are removed but will be reused, you can place them in inexpensive resealable food storage bags. Include all of the bulbs, mounting bolts, or whatever other loose items may be related to this item in the bag as well. In instances where there are multiple parts that look alike, you would do well to place a tag directly on the bag or inside of it giving the specifics of

After sanding the first layer of paint off the front fender of this early Camaro, it is quite obvious that the car has been a different color at one time. Additionally, there is evidence of some body filler that may or may not have been applied correctly. This is a good example of why stripping to bare metal is a good idea if you do not know the full history of the vehicle.

this particular component. Other labels such as "left tail-light" or "1 of 4," "2 of 4," etc., will help to make correct reassembly easier. Of course, any of these labels or notes could be referenced in your disassembly notes that you made when you were first ripping them off the vehicle.

Some components will not fit into food storage bags, but you can use the same methodology to store these parts in small storage boxes. You can find new storage boxes in a variety of sizes at your local office supply store. Cardboard can work, but plastic storage containers may be more convenient, as they are sturdier, more stackable, and can have transparent sides so you see easily what each contains. You can mark the ends too, naturally.

Large Parts

Larger components such as fenders, hoods, and doors obviously will not fit into bags or boxes. These items will need to be set on the floor or a shelf in a manner that will prevent them from falling and causing damage to themselves or other components—or people. They should also be situated so that they are easy to get to and move when you are ready for them. If a part requires two people to move it, place it where two people can get to it to avoid damage to the part or injury to yourself or others.

If possible, reinstall all mounting hardware in the component to which it belongs, or place the mounting hardware in a bag or box and label it accordingly. Again, reference this storage info with your disassembly notes to avoid last-minute trips to the hardware store scrounging up mounting bolts during the reassembly process.

STRIPPING

I know this stripper in Southern Indiana that I have visited a few times and paid a fair amount of money to. There are some things that a man needs that simply call for a stripper. Now before you get me in trouble with my spouse, let me clarify that I am of course talking about paint and rust removal from my Model A Tudor and an old Chevy truck.

Stripping is an important process in auto restoration, but it arises in collision work, too. In the former case it is often a means to getting deep into crevices and removing all rust. For collision repairs, stripping is used when a replacement panel has a finish incompatible with the rest of the vehicle's paint, or when the replacement itself has some rust. Sometimes stripping is insurance with a panel of unknown background; it is better to get it down to bare metal than paint over something that hides a poor repair or is contaminated with a troublesome chemical like silicone that will interfere with proper dispersion and adhesion of your finish coats.

One of the benefits of lacquer paint was that it could be applied in infinite coats to achieve some of the deepest, shiniest paint jobs ever seen. This was all well and good on vehicles that were used only on the show car circuit. However, whenever those multiple coats of lacquer were exposed to the elements for a significant amount of time, they would begin to look like a sunburned alligator skin. To repaint a vehicle in this situation, it is an absolute must to remove everything this side of bare metal. Lacquer paint is all but extinct now, but there are countless vehicles out there in barns and garages that have been painted with lacquer and are more than suitable for restoration.

It can be difficult to distinguish between surface rust and rust-through when looking at a potential hot rod or restoration project. The only real way to tell what's good and what isn't is to strip down to bare metal. Then you can see if you can install a patch panel to resurrect the piece or if you will be required to replace the entire piece. Of course, depending on how obvious the rust is and the availability of a patch panel, you may be better off saving your money and purchasing a new panel.

There are three basic methods used for stripping paint and rust from automobiles. In no particular order, they are media blasting, chemical stripping, and grinding or sanding. Each has its benefits and drawbacks, related expenses, and horror stories.

Media Blasting

For a long time, coarse river sand was used extensively for media blasting, hence the now outdated term "sand blasting." Sand can be, and is still, used for removing graffiti from steel bridges, masonry structures, and various other applications. However, sand can quickly put heavy scratches into something lighter and will produce significant heat, causing sheet-metal panels to warp. Silica sand is much finer than river sand, although it has drawbacks as well. Using any kind of sand for blasting purposes will create an extremely fine dust, which with prolonged exposure is known to cause silicosis, a potentially disabling inflammation of the lungs. This extremely nasty side effect can be avoided by using any of a number of alternative products.

In lieu of sand blasting, a great way to remove paint, peeling chrome, and rust is by media blasting. However, you cannot simply start blasting away at your parts. You must secure and make use of proper safety apparel, including eye and respiratory protection. There are three additional very important things to remember when media blasting: (1) mask the area that should not be blasted; (2) use the appropriate blasting media; and (3) remove all of the blasting media when the job is complete.

Masking

No matter what type of media is being used, media blasting will leave a slightly textured surface. For this reason, machined surfaces, bearing surfaces, threaded areas, or any other areas that would be negatively affected by this should be masked off. Exterior threads such as those on the back of some trim pieces can easily be protected from blasting by covering them with a length of appropriately sized rubber hose or tubing. Other areas can be masked with heavy cardboard and masking tape, accompanied by prudent use of lower blasting pressure and a careful aim.

Media Selection

Blasting media must be compatible with the material upon which it is being used. If the blasting media is harder than the surface being prepped, you will do more harm than good by hurling hard objects at it. A large volume of softer material passing by the surface is a more appropriate way of freeing the surface of unwanted material, such as paint or rust. These softer materials typically include silica sand, aluminum oxide, plastic media, or walnut shells. You should avoid using steel-shot media or coarse river sand.

Various materials other than sand are available for use in media blasting. No one material is the best for all stripping or clean-up operations, so be sure to match the media with the task. For removing paint and rust from steel, aluminum oxide is a good choice. A little more expensive is plastic media, which is best for stripping paint from metal, as it doesn't get as hot or cause warping. Although it is not the best media for any particular clean-up project, glass bead blasting does a good job on almost any surface. For cleaning soft metals such as aluminum, die cast, or brass, aluminum shot is best, although it is more expensive.

When choosing a blasting media, you must remember that any scratches or abrasions that you put into the metal while blast-cleaning will also need to be taken out. An aggressive media will no doubt remove paint and other finishes faster, but if the media is harder than the material that is being blasted, you will end up creating more work for yourself later.

The following chart gives media and air pressure recommendations for various blasting projects.

Blast Media	Surface Material	Type of Blasting	Recommended Air Pressure (psi)
Glass Bead	Aluminum, Brass, Die Cast	Cleaning	60
Aluminum Oxide	Steel	Removal of rust and paint; to increase adhesion of paint or powder coating	80–90
Silicon Carbide	Steel	Preparation for welding	80–90
Walnut Shells	Engine/Transmission Assemblies	Cleaning	80
Plastic Media	Sheet Metal	Paint removal	30–90
Aluminum Shot	Aluminum, Brass, Die Cast	Cleaning	80–90

This table serves as a handy guide to what media should be used on various materials and the recommended air pressure to use.

Media Removal

In addition to the flaking rust, paint, or whatever was on the part prior to blasting, you must also remove all of the blasting media when the blasting is finished. Much of the media used for blasting is recycled and used again, so even if your parts were not oily or greasy, previously blasted parts may have been. Any oil that is present on your parts will cause adhesion problems, so it is imperative that all parts be cleaned thoroughly after being media blasted.

A drawback to media blasting is that the media can be difficult to remove from confined areas. It is fine for use on a simple two-sided surface such as a fender. However, on a door shell, pickup truck cab, or passenger car body, some of the media will collect between panels and will be difficult to remove. If the media would stay in hiding, it might not present much of a problem, but it will most likely decide to come out when you are in the middle of spraying the perfect topcoat of paint. Years ago, I had the cab of a 1951 Chevrolet pickup sandblasted. In those particular trucks, the roof area is double-wall construction, but the back panel is single wall. Long story made short, lots of very fine sand found its way between the roof panels. Since I never got around to finishing the interior, nothing kept all of that sand in the roof. As a result, I got a light sprinkling in the cab almost every time I hit a bump in the road.

This sports car body has been stripped of all paint, most likely by some sort of media blasting. The interior has been masked off and the body is ready for an application of self-etching or epoxy primer to protect it from rust. For the body to be chemically dipped, it would need to be removed from the chassis/suspension. The body would then be primed prior to being reinstalled on the chassis.

Chemical Stripping

Chemical removal of paint and rust can be done at home or commercially. The amount of stripping to be done and the availability of a chemical stripper in your area will most likely be the determining points to consider. If you have several parts or a number of large pieces that need to be stripped, it will be more practical to have them stripped commercially. If you simply need to strip one or two pieces or just one salvage yard fender for instance, you can do this yourself.

Chemical stripping does not work well on thick plastic body filler, so if you have a panel that you know contains body filler, you should remove as much as possible before attempting to strip it chemically. A simple method of doing this is with a 36-grit disc on an orbital sander. If thick body filler is not removed before the panel is chemically stripped, the filler will begin to peel, but will not come off completely. It will proceed to prevent the stripper from actually stripping the surface beneath the filler, making the entire process a waste of time.

Regardless of brand, paint stripper in general is some pretty nasty stuff. So, be sure to follow all safety precautions on the label of the product. As someone who has stripped a complete pickup truck by hand with paint stripper, I strongly recommend that you wear rubber gloves, a respirator, thick shoes or boots, long pants, and a long-sleeved shirt. If you were to drop a glob of paint stripper on some bare skin, you will quickly wish that you hadn't. Fortunately, it only burns for a while . . . At the absolute minimum, cover as much of your skin as possible and wear long rubber gloves.

The one thing that the instructions for paint stripper do not tell you is that you should scuff the painted surface with 36- or 50-grit sandpaper prior to applying paint stripper. If you are dealing with decently applied paint, it becomes a standoff between the paint and the stripper if the surface has not been scuffed to allow the stripper to penetrate and do its work. Scuffing the surface first will allow you to use less stripper and save time in the actual stripping process.

When using paint stripper, the vehicle or parts should be on a concrete surface that can be hosed down with water after the stripping process. Check with your source of paint stripper for recommendations on disposal of the used stripper that will be rinsed from the parts.

After scuffing the painted surface, spread the paint stripper on with a paintbrush. Then wait while the stripper works its way through the multiple layers of paint and primer. As the paint begins to bubble up, use a metal scraper or razor blade to peel the softened paint from the surface. Additional paint stripper can be applied to stubborn spots. When all of the paint is removed from the panel, you must neutralize the stripper before proceeding with bodywork or applications of body filler or primer. Unless the particular stripper you are using calls for a different method of neutralization, use lots of water. However, you must contain the runoff and dispose of it properly and according to local codes.

Although I would not attempt to strip a complete car or truck by hand ever again, any one part is considerably smaller and therefore less involved. If you have the need to remove paint from one fender or a smaller panel, using a gallon of paint stripper is an effective method for the do-it-yourselfer.

Commercial Dipping

If you have numerous parts or large pieces (including complete body shells) to be stripped, having them dipped commercially is the practical way to go. The pieces and parts should be disassembled as completely as possible and any large amounts of body filler removed for the best results. Large parts are dipped individually, while small parts are placed into a basket and then dipped.

The parts being stripped first go into a "hot tank" that is filled with a caustic solution. This removes wax, grease, and paint from the metal. This step requires four to eight hours, depending on the amount of buildup on the metal. When the wax, grease, and paint is gone, the metal is removed from the "hot tank" and rinsed with plain water for three to four hours to remove all of the caustic solution.

The next step places the metal parts into a second vat that is filled with de-rusting solution. While in this solution to remove rust, the material is connected to an electrical charge. Unlike chrome plating and powder coating, which use an electric charge to draw chromium molecules or powder material to the metal, the de-rusting process reverses the current. Iron oxide molecules (rust) are drawn away from the part, leaving good metal. Depending on the condition of the metal and the amount of rust, this step may take 20 to 40 hours. When the remaining metal is removed from the de-rusting vat, the parts are thoroughly rinsed again with plain water to neutralize any remaining de-rusting solution.

Parts that are chemically stripped should be primed with epoxy primer as soon as practical to prevent the for-

A dual action (DA) sander has been a staple of the bodywork business for a very long time. Depending on the grit of the sanding disc that is used, it will quickly remove paint and primer from an area to be repaired or excess body filler from an area that is being filled.

mation of surface rust. A benefit or drawback of chemical dipping is that the stripping solution will get to all surfaces of the parts that are immersed. This will remove all rust, but may leave areas of good metal with no protection if you cannot access them to apply epoxy primer and paint or undercoating.

Grinding/Sanding

If you simply need to get down to bare metal in a localized area on a few parts, an electric or pneumatic orbital sander will do the job quite sufficiently. By using a 36-grit sanding disc, you can remove old body filler or previous layers of paint and primer very quickly and exactly where you desire. You can often finish this in less time than what it would take for you to load the parts in a truck to transport them to a media blaster or chemical stripping facility.

However, you should limit this method to relatively small localized areas, as the process produces lots of heat that can cause otherwise perfectly good panels to begin warping. You should not attempt to remove paint from an entire vehicle with a sander. You would no doubt create enough heat to cause significant warping; you would go through several sanding discs; and this process would take too much time. Even when used to strip a small area, the sanding disc should be moved around, as opposed to simply holding the sander in one spot. You should also hold the sander so that the sanding disc flexes slightly, rather than flat against the surfaces being stripped.

CHAPTER 5
COLLISION REPAIR—METAL

Repairing dented or bent sheetmetal components is a relatively simple five-step process. Remove the paint from the area that requires repair, straighten the deformed sheet metal as much as possible, apply a skim coat of filler to perfect the surface shape, prime, and then paint. (See Chapter 7 for rust repair.)

PANEL REPAIR

In theory, dent repair is very simple. However, inexperienced body workers often make the job more difficult than it needs to be. The misguided reasoning goes like this: it took a major impact to make a big, deep dent, so it must take a big hammer slug to straighten it out. The body worker then picks up the biggest, heaviest hammer from the tool chest and proceeds to wale the tar out of the damaged sheet metal from the opposite side. Now admittedly, it may require a big hammer and a couple of hefty swings, but if you don't know what you are doing, you are more than likely going to create more damage.

The correct way to remove a dent is to "undo" the damage—that is, hammer the dent out in the opposite progression of the way that it happened. On a simple dent, such as a baseball hitting the middle of a panel, this is a simple task to undo. When two vehicles collide, or a tree or utility pole jumps out in front of your car, dents become much more complex. During the initial impact, sheet metal is pushed inward. Since it is a formed piece that has been stamped into a predetermined shape (such as a fender), it already has some forces built in. When these forces are combined with the force of the impact, the sheet metal surrounding the initial point of contact typically bulges outward as a reactionary force. In this simple example, the process would be to hammer the bulging sheet metal back into place, and then hammer the dented sheet metal back out from the inside or pull it back out from the outside.

Automotive collisions typically are not that simple though, as the actual crash is rarely limited to just one point of impact. One vehicle's bumper will hit the other vehicle in a fender, while the fender of the first vehicle then hits the door of the second vehicle, or some other

similar scenario. The point is that the entire damage needs to be repaired in the reverse sequential order of how it happened. That does not mean that you must repair the door before you repair the fender, but the dents in each individual panel should be addressed in the reverse order of how they occurred. To proceed differently will create more work for you, as you will actually be stretching the metal and causing more damage.

Dolly-On/Dolly-Off Hammering

First of all, in most situations, using a hammer by itself (without a dolly behind the metal) will merely cause a larger than desired area of metal to move inward, which is not what is needed to repair the dent. By using a dolly behind the panel and a hammer in front of the panel, the

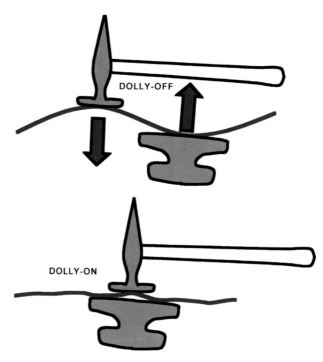

This exaggerated drawing should explain the differences between dolly-off and dolly-on hammering. The terms simply describe the relationship between the position of the body hammer and the body dolly when striking a piece of sheet metal.

For orientation, this is the left rear wheel on a four-door sedan. The rear quarter panel and door dents each require pulling with a slide hammer and then some body filler to be added for a smooth surface. Both the wheel and tire need to be replaced.

This damage here is too deep to cover with filler alone, but access to the back side with a body hammer is very limited. Using a stud gun followed by a slide hammer, as described in Chapter 1, would allow these panels to be pulled back fairly close to original shape. A skim coat of plastic body filler could then be added to finish the repair prior to primer and paint.

REPAIRING A GROUP OF DENTS

In the world of auto body repair, there is everything from minor dents and dings to high-impact collisions. A majority of this damage could be repaired at home by anyone who has the desire to learn how to do it. These are the simple dents that commonly occur in parking lots, from sliding off the road on wet or icy roads, or sometimes just from not seeing something else that is in your own driveway.

Although there may be points of impact on multiple panels, no panels require replacement or realignment. They merely need to be straightened out and refinished. To get the lowdown on these common repairs, follow along as one of the body workers from Jerry's Auto Body does some metal straightening and some filling prior to prepping for paint. The dents in the doors are shallow enough to be filled, while the rear quarter needs to be straightened and then perfected with a skim coat of filler.

This Dodge sedan suffered some minor damage to the driver-side doors and rear quarter panel. None of the damage is severe, and most all of it could be repaired by the hobbyist. Careful attention to detail during the body repair and prep work will go a long way toward making this sedan look like new, once the repairs are completed.

This photo shows the original damage before any metal straightening was done. Where metal work is required and filler will be applied, the paint is removed completely with a DA sander. Outside of this area, paint is removed but the original primer or sealer is left intact. These two areas will receive the heaviest coatings of primer-surfacer, although it will be built up in thin layers, rather than one thick coat. The large gray area has been scuffed lightly to offer good adhesion.

Above: *The damage to this sedan is typical of what a hobbyist can easily repair, without getting in over your head. It consisted of a few small dents in the doors and rear quarter panel. No metal was creased or torn, and no glass was broken. Even if your sheet-metal straightening skills are not the best, most of these repairs could be filled with body filler to a satisfactory degree. A deeper dent would simply take more layers of filler, as the latter cannot be applied very thick or it will not cure properly.*

Below: *To straighten sheet metal, you often need to pull it to remove a dent. To make this easier, this stud welder is used to weld temporary small metal rods (about $\frac{1}{8}$ inch in diameter and $2\frac{1}{2}$ inches long) to the sheet metal.*

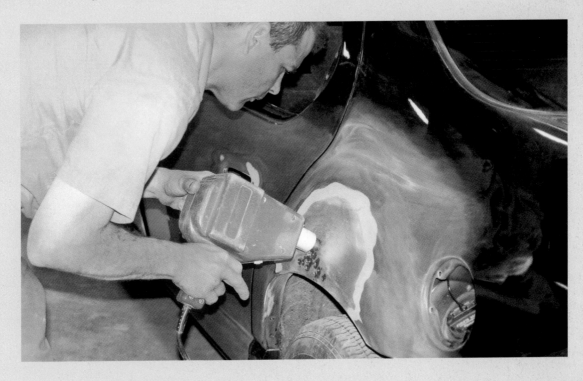

To make the studs most efficient, they should be placed in the deepest areas of the damage. Additional studs should then be placed in areas that are not as deep.

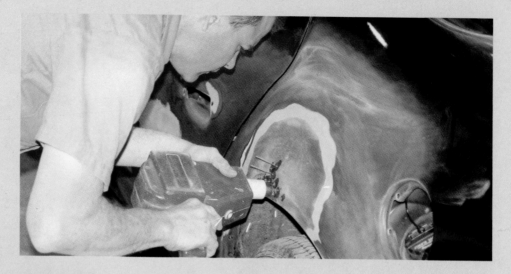

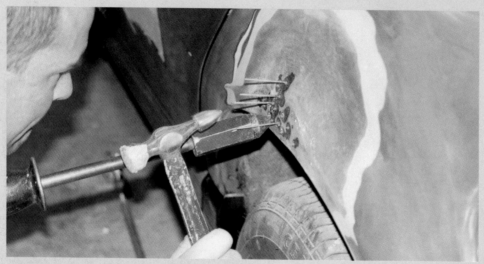

A slide hammer can then be slid over the rods one at a time, and then slid out to pull the sheet metal to its correct position. Sometimes a hammer may need to be used to tap the metal back in slightly if it was pulled out too far.

The slide hammer is moved to the next rod, and then pulled out, to undo the effects of the impact. Learning how to read dents and knowing where to pull is an art that takes practice. Typically, the deepest portion of the dent is pulled out first and then lesser dents are worked. As long as none of the studs are removed, you can go back and pull previously pulled studs more if necessary. If this were a "compound dent," in which the metal had bulged outward at the sides of the dent, you would pound in the bulge first before pulling the impact dent.

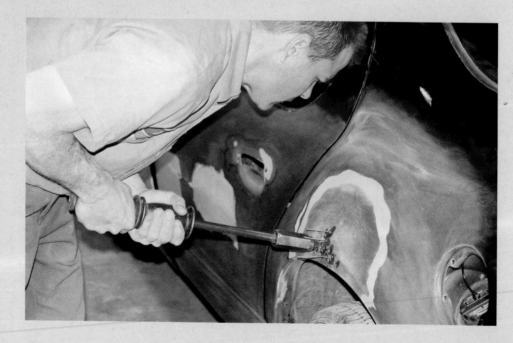

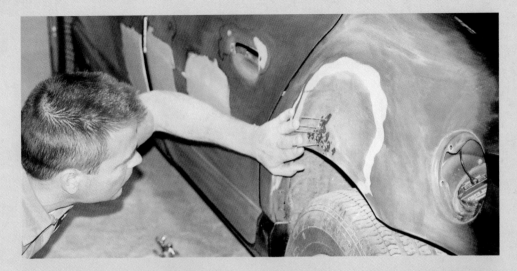

After some pulling, the body worker checks the progress to verify that the panel has been returned to its proper contour. You want to return the panel as closely as possible to its original shape; however, you do not want any of the panel to be too high. High spots will need to be hammered back down (prior to application of filler), while subtle low spots can be filled.

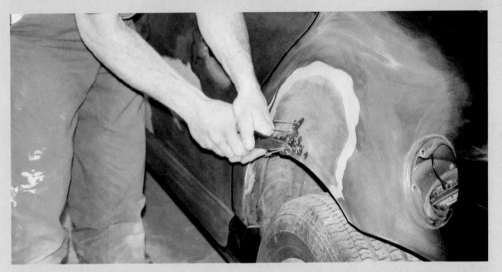

With the pulling completed, the rods can be cut off as close to the body as possible with a pair of diagonal cutters.

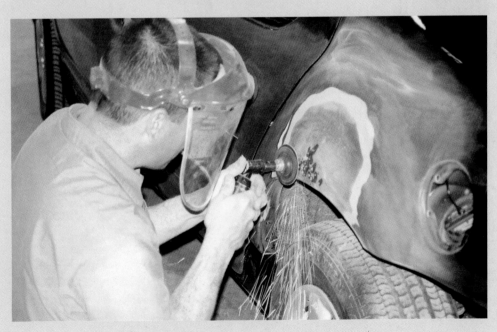

The stubs are then ground away with a grinder and a coarse disc.

The lip of the fender has been determined to be slightly low, so it is pulled out by using the slide hammer and a fender lip attachment.

A couple of more tugs with the slide hammer and it should be pretty close.

A slight high spot is finessed back into place with the use of a small hammer. Older vehicles generally have thicker sheet metal, while newer vehicles generally have thinner, more pliable sheet metal. The amount of brute strength and finesse necessary will depend largely on the vintage of the vehicle.

Prior to the application of any body filler, the various layers of sheet metal, primer, and paint are quite evident on the rear quarter panel of this sedan. The very smallest dark area is where small rods were temporarily welded to the panel so that the slide hammer could be used to straighten the dent. The next larger area is where the paint has been sanded off to expose bare metal. Outside of that is the original primer or sealer used beneath the factory paint. Next is the paint that has been scuffed to enhance adhesion of the primer-surfacer, and finally there is the untouched original painted surface.

A mixing board with disposable tear-off sheets is great for mixing body filler. Appropriate amounts of filler and hardener are mixed together using a plastic spreader. After the filler is spread, that sheet is torn off and disposed of, which provides a clean surface for mixing the next batch of filler.

Using a flexible spreader and a careful eye, the filler is spread to fill any low spots. Care must be taken to minimize air bubbles. When the filler hardens, it can then be sanded to its final shape with 80- or 100-grit sandpaper.

After using a slide hammer to straighten the metal to very near its original contour, two or three thin coats of body filler are applied to match the final contour. If pinholes are present after sanding the body filler, glazing putty can be used to fill them.

The areas of body filler show that the actual damaged areas to this sedan were really four small dents (two in each driver-side door) and a larger dent above the left rear wheel. If they were repainted separately, this car would look like a spotted leopard, so the entire side will be repainted.

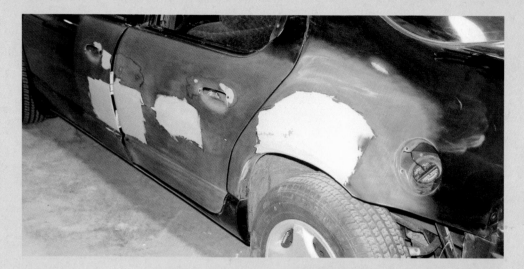

The doors on this sedan are relatively straight front to back, while contoured from top to bottom. To maintain this straightness, a long sanding board is used to sand in a front to back direction, while moving up and down along the door.

Due to the irregular pressure of your hand, you should not sand without using some type of a sanding block. Using your hand alone will tend to make the panel wavy, as more pressure will be applied by your fingers and less in the area in between them. However, checking your progress while sanding by taking the time to feel the sanded panel with your hand will give a good indication of high and low spots.

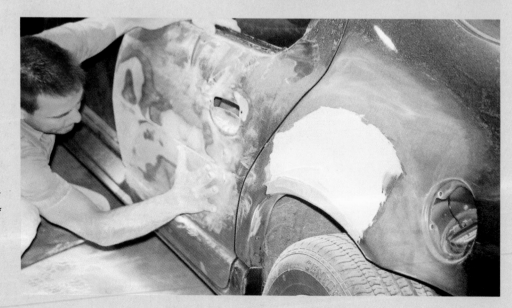

Be sure to use an air hose occasionally to remove any buildup of body filler dust.

To merely scuff existing paint or as a final smoothing effort, Scotch-Brite pads may be used. Available in three different levels of coarseness, the coarsest would be appropriate for scuffing paint before applying a sealer. The finest would be more appropriate for final smoothing prior to applying primer-surfacer.

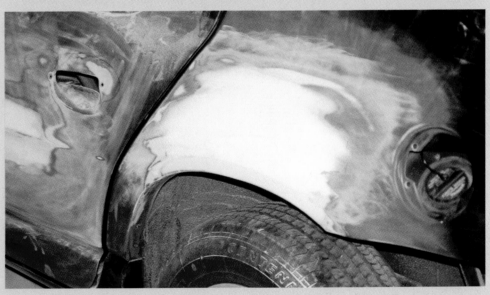

Looking at this filled area after the sanding has been completed, we can tell that filler (pale yellow in color) was used to cover the larger area, and a slight amount of glaze (light blue in color) was used to finish the edge of the wheelwell.

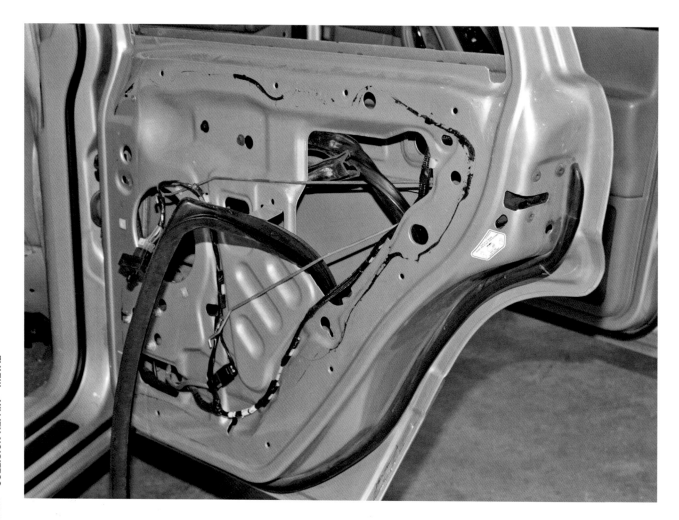

This door has already been repaired, but the glass needs to be reinstalled, the window riser mechanism connected, and the interior panel installed. The thick black rubber is actually a portion of the molding that fits around the glass, but has simply been stuck inside the door for safekeeping until the glass is reinstalled. Keeping track of parts during repair is important.

sheet metal can be worked in a more predictable manner, as the dolly focuses the force of the hammer.

Dollies are used in two basic ways: dolly on or dolly off. When hammering *on* the dolly, the dolly is located behind the sheet metal and directly beneath the hammer blow. This method is used to knock down high spots or to smooth ripples within the relatively small size of the dolly. Hammering *off* the dolly is done by hitting the surface of the panel adjacent to the dolly, rather than on it. This causes the dolly to push outward while the hammer pushes inward and is typically used on larger areas of repair.

Door Repair

Any time when a door is damaged in a collision, the person making the repair may have to deal with more than just damaged sheet metal. Just by the very nature of the door being a movable component, you may be required to replace, repair, or at a minimum adjust the hinges or the latch mechanisms. Additionally, broken door glass may potentially have to be removed and replaced, as well as window riser mechanisms. That may be it on a barebones automobile, but on higher level vehicles, there is also the potential for damage to door mounted remote controls, stereo speakers, and now more commonly to side-curtain airbags. Of course, if the exterior of the door is damaged sufficiently, the interior door panel may be damaged as well. None of these additional tasks are beyond home repair; they simply add opportunities to gain firsthand knowledge.

Doors and Door Skins

Since automobile doors consist of two basic components—a mostly hollow inner panel and an outer skin—some door repairs can be made by simply re-skinning the door. There are some things that you should consider before going this route, however. First and foremost, this repair will be beneficial only if the original inner panel is still undamaged (or at least straight). If collision impact caused damage to the inner panel that cannot be easily repaired, you will get a better result with a replacement door. Likewise, if the outer skin is damaged due to rust, you should verify that the inner panel is still structurally sound. It may be usable, but then again it might actually be in worse shape than the outer skin, as manufacturers vary widely in the amount of paint they apply to unexposed or inaccessible surfaces.

If the inner panel is still usable, you will need to determine if an outer skin is available for your vehicle's make and model. If it is, you are in luck as a door skin will be considerably less expensive than a replacement door. Of course, depending on whether this is your daily driver or a ground-up restoration, you may choose to replace the entire door while you are at it.

If you decide to replace the door skin, it can be done as follows. To make the work easier, remove the door from the vehicle, remove the internal components from the inside of the door, and then set the door atop a pair of sawhorses or other suitable work stand.

The original door skin is secured by its edges wrapped around the flange of the inner door panel. To remove it, use a grinder along the edge of the door to separate the main part of the door skin from the part that it flaps over. When this is completed, you should be able to remove the skin. If it cannot be removed, there may be spot welds around the flange that you will need to drill out. You will also need to remove the part that flaps over from the inside of the inner door panel. Depending on its condition, you may want to have the inner door media blasted or dipped to remove any rust after the outer skin has been removed. If you do this first step, you should follow it up with a couple of coats of epoxy primer.

To install a new skin, you should first double-check to make sure that no fragments of the previous door skin, spot welds, or panel adhesive remain on the surface to which the new skin will be applied. Then position the new skin in place so that the excess "skin" is centered front to back, and top to bottom. Using a permanent marker or a scribe, make some positioning reference marks on the inside of the door skin so that you can place it in this position again. Then remove the door skin, apply a bead of panel adhesive to the inside of the door skin and to the mating surface on the inner door panel. Allow the panel adhesive to get slightly tacky, and then press the door skin into position.

Use C-clamps, clamping pliers (Vise-Grips), or other types to secure the door skin in place. Take the appropriate precautions to make sure that you do not damage the new door skin or inner panel. After the two panels are clamped together, wipe away any excess panel adhesive that oozes from inside the door.

After the panel adhesive has set (refer to the product label), the edges of the door skin will still need to be folded over the edge of the inner door panel. There are several ways to do this and even more tools available to use for this task. Some body workers use door skinning pliers to fold the edge over, while others use duckbill locking pliers. After the edge is folded over somewhat, you must press it down flat against the inside of the door panel. Some body workers use a light, door skinning hammer, while others use a mallet or a smoothed face body hammer and a dolly. This is one of those cases where there are several ways to do the same task, depending on what tools are available to you and how you use them. The main thing to remember is that the edge of the door skin must be flat against the inner panel, but you don't want to do any damage to the outer side.

Hinges

Although some vehicles may have three hinges on each door, two hinges per door is more common. Regardless of the number of hinges, the pivot point for all hinges must be aligned for the door to operate properly. If any of the hinges have become misaligned during an accident (or possibly due to rust if the vehicle has been sitting around for quite awhile), the door simply will not open and close as it should.

If you have established that one of the hinges is misaligned, you will need to determine which half of it needs repair or adjustment. Half of the hinge attaches to the door, while the other half attaches to the door pillar. If the latter appears not to be damaged, but the door itself has suffered an impact, the door half of the hinge would be suspect. Conversely, if the door is unscathed, but the door pillar has sustained damage, you will most likely need to repair or adjust the hinge at the door pillar.

On most, but certainly not all vehicles, the door pillar portion of the hinge has less adjustability. Any adjustability is limited to moving the door surface closer to, or farther away from, the vehicle's centerline (right or left). The door half of the hinge typically has the most adjustability, as the mounting holes in the hinge are slotted. This allows the door to be moved up, down, forward or backward, but not left or right. If you are lucky, the door mounting bolts may

REPLACING A DOOR SKIN

To see how an old door skin is removed and a replacement installed, I visited Morfab Customs where Chris was in the process of re-skinning an early Camaro door. The process sounds more difficult than it actually is and is oftentimes a much better method of repairing a damaged door.

Right: *A replacement door skin for this vehicle costs about $100, while a replacement door costs around five times that much from the same source. Since the need for this repair is rust-through due to some amateur bodywork in the past, a replacement door skin is the feasible way to go.*

Below: *To remove a door skin, you should use a grinder with a 36- or 80-grit disc to grind through the edge of the door skin. You should not grind the face of the door or the flap that is folded over, but the very edge. This will quickly separate the skin from the door.*

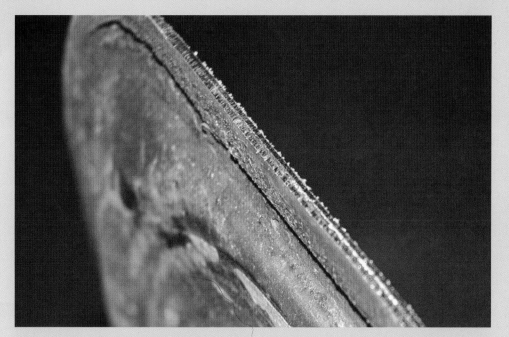

With the door skin separated at the door's edge, the skin can be removed from the outside of the door and the flap can be removed from the inside of the inner door panel. It may be necessary to drill out spot welds from some doors to remove the skin. With the door skin separated at the edge, the skin will now be ready to be removed.

Now is the time to have the inner door panel media blasted or chemically dipped to remove any rust, and then follow this up with a coat of epoxy primer. The door shown here is solid, but lots of surface rust is apparent. Between removing the skin and replacing it is the only time when you can effectively do any surface treatment to the inside of the door.

The replacement skin will be glued in place and then the edges of the skin wrapped around the inner panel, much like it was originally. For the glue to form a good bond, the mating area of the inner panel is scuffed with an angle head grinder to remove any paint or rust.

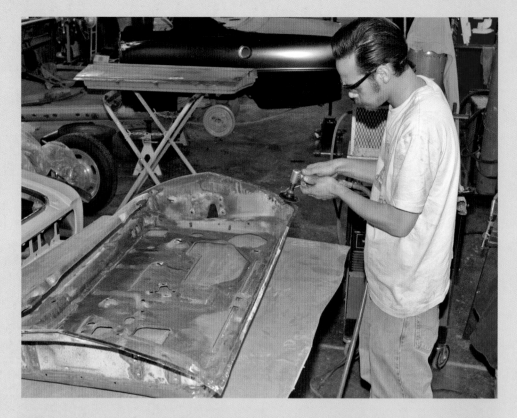

Likewise, the mating surface of the replacement skin is scuffed in similar fashion. The original doors did not use glue to attach the door skins, but it does make for a better repair.

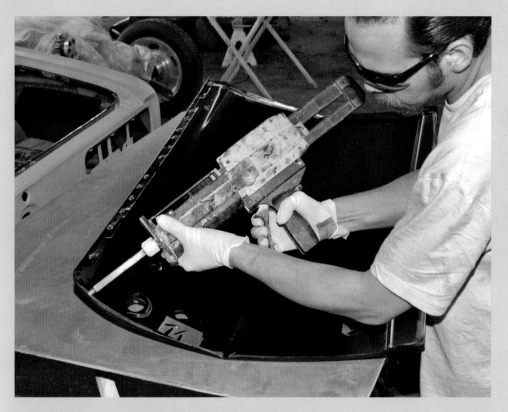

The glue used for securing a door skin is 3M's Door Skin Adhesive—pretty simple, huh? It is a two-part epoxy that requires a specialized application gun that mixes the two parts as they are dispensed. Since the two parts are not mixed until they are used, the product has a longer shelf life.

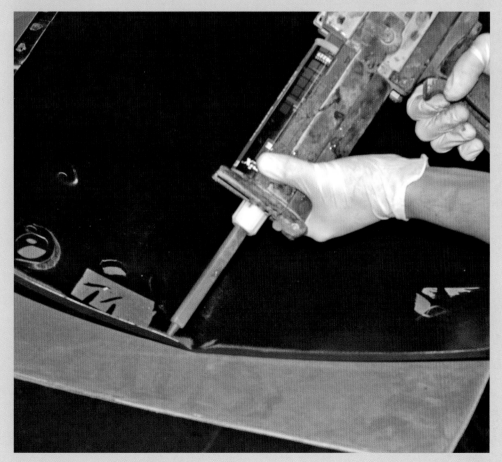

Using the gun much like a caulking gun for chores around the house, Chris begins at the top of one side of the replacement door skin and works his way down that side.

Chris then continues across the bottom of the door skin, all the time making sure that the adhesive is applied to the surface that will abut the inner panel.

A bead approximately ¼ inch wide is basically centered on the door skin where the surface has been scuffed previously.

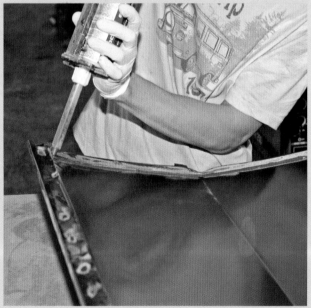

Chris continues to apply the adhesive to the top of the opposite side of the door from where he started. The lip that does not have any adhesive applied actually fits over a portion of the inner door panel.

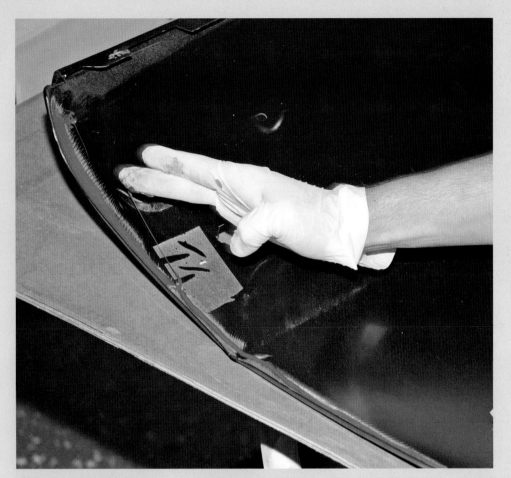

To avoid contaminating the adhesive with oils from his fingertips, Chris puts on a disposable glove and then uses his fingertips to spread the adhesive.

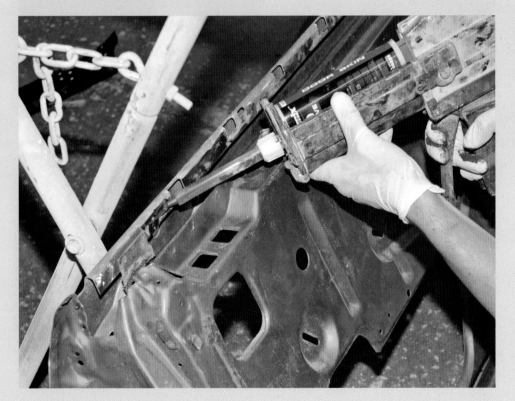

Chris then applies a bit of adhesive on the lip of the inner door panel where the outer door skin will lap over.

Right: *With the door skin exterior side facing down and sitting on a suitable work surface, the inner door panel is slid into place. Make sure that the inner door panel is positioned as far into the door skin as possible, and is centered front to back.*

Below: *The previous steps are not required if you are not using adhesive to secure the door. With the door skin and the inner door panel adequately positioned in relation to each other, the tedious portion of the repair begins— hammering the edges of the outer door skin over the edge and flat.*

At this point, portions of the door skin are at about 90 degrees to the flange that they will be hammered over, while other areas are at about 180 degrees.

Prior to hammering any of the edge over the flange, the door skin should be clamped in place with as many clamps as you have available. The adhesive is still pliable at this time, and you definitely do not want the door skin moving in relation to the inner door panel.

At the minimum, try to clamp the door skin to the inner panel at the four corners. You may have to move some of the clamps while hammering, so having multiple clamps in use will help to prevent movement between the two panels.

Besides preventing movement between the two panels, the clamps hold the two pieces together tighter, allowing you to fold the edge over tighter and therefore providing a better seam.

Chris will be using a hammer-on dolly approach for folding the door skin edge over the inner door panel flange. In other words, he will be hammering directly onto the dolly, with the two panels in between.

To minimize marring of the new door skin, Chris has wrapped a shop towel tightly around the dolly. When skinning a door, you do not want the dolly to have any effect on the door skin, but the dolly is required so that the hammer does not simply bounce off the door panels. The shop towel provides some padding to prevent marring, but still provides a solid surface to hammer against.

Chris works his way around the door skin, hammering the edge over slightly with each pass. You should avoid attempting to hammer the door skin edge over completely all at once.

You will notice that Chris' hammer has one end that is straight and another that is curved. This curved end allows the user to strike the surface at a perpendicular angle when in tight situations.

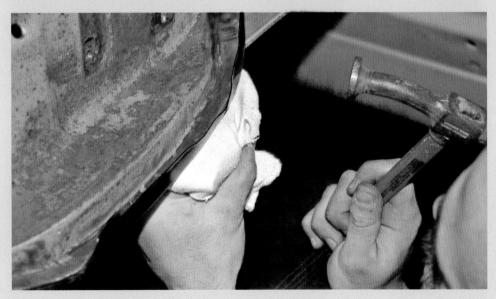

The curved end may also be useful where there is ample room, but the positioning of the work piece and the body worker is at an angle that may require extra effort using the straight end of the hammer.

Above: *With each pass around the door, the skin is folded over a little more.*

Right: *Clearly in this photo, the edge of the door skin is closer to being flat and flush with the inner door panel. To avoid damage to the door skin, several relatively light taps are more productive than fewer heavier hits. Finesse is one of the secrets to successful bodywork and metal working.*

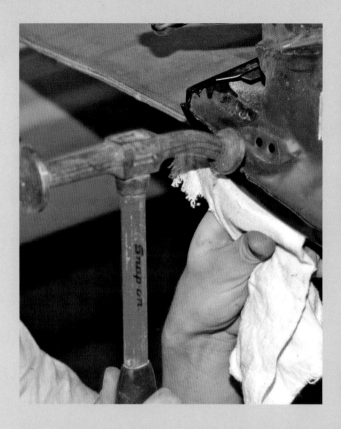

Working around the corners of the door will require a little more effort to get the desired result.

Chris keeps the shop towel tightly wrapped around the dolly to help minimize damage to the outside of the door skin.

Special attention will be required where the door changes shape. You will need to bend the metal over gradually to each side of the contour change to ensure a good fit. Take your time, use finesse, and you will learn how to maneuver through these areas like a pro.

Take your time to make sure that the door skin edge is hammered as flat as possible against the inside of the inner door panel. If it is not flat, it will look funny and unprofessional, and may create a hard-to-paint spot that will collect moisture and promote rust.

Coming down the back stretch, this door skin installation is almost finished. Chris has installed lots of door skins, but the process still takes about an hour, so it will most likely take longer for a novice.

After completing all of the hammering, install as many clamps as possible so that the adhesive cures evenly. The 3M Door Skin Adhesive will require about four hours to cure completely.

Below: *This is the door for the opposite side of the vehicle. Chris had re-skinned it earlier in the day. No dents, no rust, and almost ready for paint.*

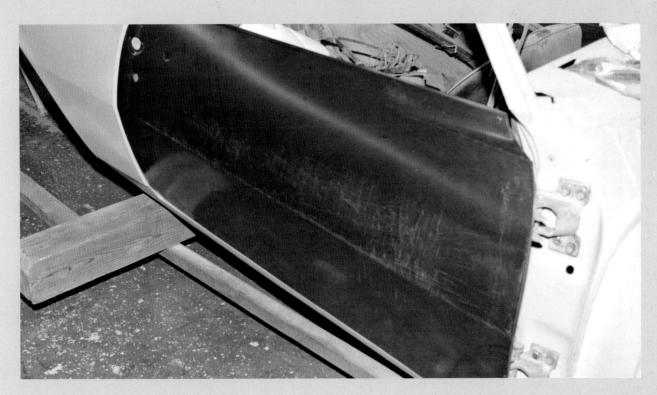

COLLISION REPAIR—METAL

79

The hinge mechanisms in most vehicles are fairly robust, making them reasonably durable during a collision. However, collision or rust damage to the cowl or B-pillar in a four-door sedan may require removal and reinstallation. This upper hinge simply bolts onto the cowl and the door, while newer versions are welded in place, thus requiring hinge pin removal to remove the door.

When you are in the process of disassembling a vehicle in preparation for making repairs, you may have to make some educated guesses about how things come apart. Most door handles attach from the inside, meaning that the interior door panel must be removed.

have just been slightly loose and the door moved slightly during impact. This will allow you to loosen the mounting bolts a bit more, adjust the door to its proper position, and then retighten the bolts.

Before attempting to align a door, you should always check the hinge pin and bushing. If there is any slop, you

This lower hinge is comparable to the upper one, except that it also includes a very stiff spring. The purpose of the spring and the notched arm to which it mounts is to hold the door open in one of two positions. Without this spring mechanism, when unlatched the door would fly open all the way (or stay closed) when parked on a hill or incline.

should replace both of them, as you will not be able to properly align the door otherwise.

If any of the door hinges are obviously damaged, you would most likely be better off replacing the hinge than attempting to repair it. What may seem like a minor misalignment at the hinge will be more pronounced at the opposite end of the door.

Latches and Actuators

If an exterior door latch is damaged, you will most likely have to remove the interior door panel to gain access to the bolt that secures the latch. However, prior to completely removing the latch from the door after removing the mounting hardware, you will need to disconnect the actuator rods or linkage. Unless the method of reassembly is obvious beyond a doubt, now would be a great time to make some notes or take some photos to aid in reassembly. A less than perfect reassembly will rear its ugly head every time you get in or out of the vehicle.

As actuators are relatively thin by design and span a large percentage of the door's width, they are susceptible to impact damage any time a door is hit. You will simply need to use your best judgment, or rely on trial and error, to assess if you can repair (straighten) a damaged actuator

With the exterior door handle off already, we can see that it attaches with two mounting screws from the inside. Whenever repairs are made to a door, it is best to remove the glass and door handles, and then repaint the entire door, rather than painting just a portion. Even if no paint is applied to the door handle or glass area, removal and replacement is typically easier than masking these areas.

rod or should purchase a new one. Although you probably would be required to purchase an entire door from your local salvage yard just to obtain the internal workings, the prudent course of action may be to replace and refinish (repaint) a good but usable door rather than attempt to repair one that has taken a direct hit.

Window Mechanisms

Other items in the door that can be damaged are the window glass, the window riser mechanism (manual or electric), and the window channel in which the glass slides. These items are more likely to require replacement rather than repair if they are damaged. Anything that may cause glass to be misaligned or in a bind will most likely cause it to break eventually, so it is better to replace the necessary parts now while the vehicle is apart, rather than to wait until later and be required to disassemble and reassemble the door again.

PANEL REPLACEMENT

If the body damage is more severe than you can repair, or you have hammered the affected panel into oblivion while attempting to straighten it, you will need to replace the damaged panel. As long as the original panel is one that can be removed from the vehicle, this is always an option.

Even a roof or quarter panel can be cut from a donor car and welded in place if necessary.

If it is not obvious how to remove a damaged panel from your vehicle, you may be forced to do what professional body workers do and simply begin removing bolts until the panel can be detached. You may be able to find the necessary info in a repair manual specific to your vehicle, but body panel removal information is usually not included in such books. As you remove the panel, make notes regarding the number and type of fasteners that you are removing so you can verify that the replacement panel is reinstalled and secured correctly. You should also make notes of any panels that overlap, and if they need to be removed and reinstalled in a specific order.

Any subassemblies that are connected to the part being replaced are usually sold separately and therefore should be removed from the original and reused if possible. If these additional parts are not usable, they will need to be replaced as well. You should not discard any panels that are being replaced until after you have made all the repairs and finished the project. Otherwise, you may be required to purchase a new widget or other seemingly insignificant component that is not included with the replacement but is a necessity for reinstallation.

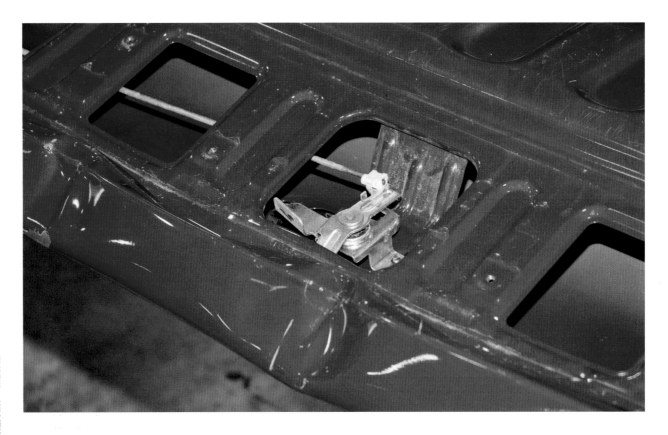

Even though this truck tailgate is going to be replaced with a new one, the latter does not include the latch mechanism, linkage, or other hardware. This latch mechanism will not be seen after the access panel is reinstalled, so if the latch works and is not damaged cosmetically on the outside, you can save some money by using the old one.

Clean the replacement panels with wax and grease remover prior to doing anything else to them. Then scuff the surface with 240-grit sandpaper so that primers and topcoats adhere properly. Consult with your auto paint supplier for its recommendations on the correct undercoat necessary to prep the panels for the paint system you will be using. Primer undercoats should be applied prior to the panel being installed on the vehicle. To allow for proper paint blending, topcoats should be applied only after the panel has been installed and aligned on the vehicle. However, some panels, such as doors and hoods, may need to be painted (at least on the edges) prior to being installed. Some of these areas are difficult to paint after installation, but will stick out like the proverbial sore thumb if not painted. Painting will be discussed in detail in Chapter 9.

PANEL ALIGNMENT

Just because you have straightened every dent, removed every ripple, and have all of the damaged panels repaired (or replaced), your job as a body worker is not finished. Prior to applying paint, you still need to make sure that all of these panels fit together as they should. Most obviously, all of the bodylines should align from one panel to the next. If any of these lines don't flow from one panel to another, it will quickly be noticeable to you, as well as others. Not quite as obvious from a distance, but just as noticeable up close, is whether the edge of each panel fits with the next. Some vehicles fit better from the factory than others, no doubt about it. How well they fit after you have painted the vehicle, however, is up to you and will be a great testimony to your attention to detail.

It may be necessary to install shims behind some panels to make them align properly with adjacent panels, whether shims were used at the factory or not. Hoods and deck lids may present the biggest problem, as any ill fit will need to be evenly split between the two sides. Doors and fenders should be fit as accurately as possible, but slight variations from one side of the car to the other will not be as noticeable as a hood or deck lid that is biased to one side or the other.

Consistency in gap width is the prime objective, while factory tolerances or tighter make for a good target. To obtain consistent gaps, you may need to remove or add

Likewise, you can reuse the latch and the cable on each end. In this case, disassembly is rather straightforward. Any time you are replacing panels (especially doors, tailgates, hood or deck lids), it is a good idea to leave the original hardware attached until you are ready to install it or replacement hardware on the new panel. An air ratchet or drill makes quick work of removing or reinstalling fasteners used to hold body panels and their hardware together, but hand tools are less expensive.

Whenever you are working with linkages, or anything that is similar but different, from one side or the other, make sure that you label it somehow. A little time spent labeling will be much easier than installing the piece in the wrong place and having to disassemble and reinstall it later.

material to a panel. Although it is not always possible, gaps that are the thickness of a paint stir stick is a common goal among body workers.

If you remove a panel from the vehicle to make repairs, you should reinstall it prior to adding any body filler to verify that the latter will not cause panel alignment problems. Any panels where body filler has been applied are suspect when gaps are too tight, because getting the surface smooth may have required too much buildup. This usually happens when a portion of the area being filled was actually higher than it should have been and the surrounding area is brought out to an incorrect surface height.

LIGHTS

Whenever a vehicle is in a collision, you should verify two things afterward: do the lights still function and do the lenses require replacement? This admittedly is a low priority in the big scheme of things, but you don't want to find out that your headlights don't work when you are driving at night and are away from home. Verifying that the lights work is easy to do; simply start the vehicle, check the turn signals, the headlights (high beam and low beam), and the brake lights. You will need to check lights at both the front and back of the vehicle. An extra person will save you a few laps around the vehicle, but you can do it by your-

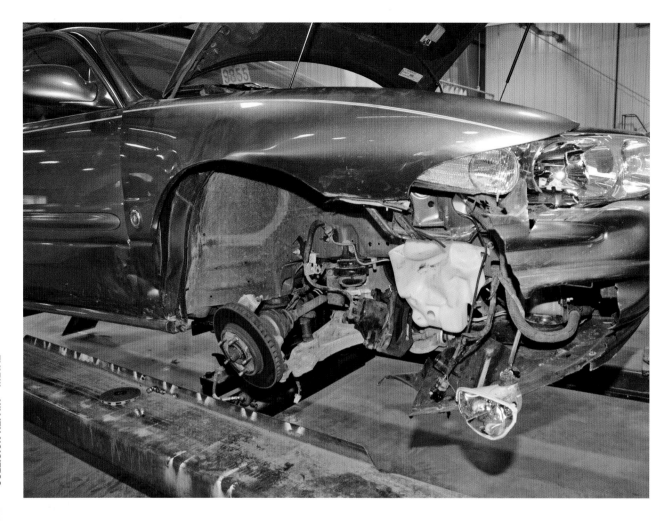

Seeing the big picture of the damage makes repairing it much easier, or at least makes it more apparent as to what needs to be done. On this Buick sedan, the right front wheel and tire assembly was pushed backward, causing the front fender to move toward the rear.

self. To check the brake lights by yourself, back toward a vertical surface, stopping within a foot or two away from it. With the vehicle stopped, keep your foot on the brake pedal and look in your inside rearview mirror. Unless there is an abundance of ambient light, you should be able to see the reflection from the brake lights on the vertical surface. If not, the brake lights may not be working or you simply can't see them. In this case, enlist the help of a second person to verify whether they are working or not.

For any lights that do not work, check first to make sure that the bulb is fully plugged in, as it could have been jarred loose in the accident. Then check to see if the bulb is burned out (may have some discoloration) or possibly broken and replace if necessary. If these checks do not provide a reason for malfunction, check the appropriate fuse. If it is blown, replace it with the appropriate size and amperage. If none of these actions correct the problem, you most likely have a wiring problem. This could be a broken wire, a damaged light socket, or a ground wire has come loose.

If any of the light lenses are cracked or broken, they should be replaced, as they cannot be repaired. You can purchase new lenses at the car dealer, some auto parts stores, or from a salvage yard. Prices will vary, so you will have to decide between taking the time to find what you need and paying a little more for the convenience of taking it home that day. Note that even though a cracked lens may look OK and the light may still work, if you don't replace it, the housing can take on water and create problems.

Headlights

Many vehicles have headlight systems that turn the lights on automatically based upon ambient light. If your vehicle is equipped with this type of headlight switch, you may need to turn the switch to the manual setting to verify that the headlights actually work.

Another concern with headlights is that they are aimed correctly. This is not as important on newer vehicles that have a replaceable bulb that is installed into the back of the headlamp assembly. However, on vehicles that use sealed beam headlights, they should be aimed as accurately as possible.

To check the aim of your headlights, you need between 35 and 40 feet of uniformly sloped driving area and a wall. The driving surface does not have to be level, so your driveway and garage door may work. Park your vehicle so that the headlights are from 2 to 3 feet from the wall and turn on the low beam headlights. With some tape that can be easily removed, outline the bright spots of each headlight on the wall. Now back the vehicle straight back so that the headlights are now about 25 feet away from the wall. (Mind what's behind you as you back up!) Turn the low

beam headlights on again if you turned them off. The top of the low beam shining on the wall should be no higher than the top marks on the wall or lower than the center of the original area. Adjust as necessary and repeat the aiming process until the lights are dialed in.

BUMPERS

By design, bumpers should take the brunt of most damage in a vehicle collision. Sometimes they do, sometimes they do not, but that is beside the point. What you are concerned with is how to repair or replace one if the bumper on your vehicle is damaged. Whether your bumper is chrome plated or painted will have a direct impact (pun fully intended) on the method of repair.

Bumper Removal

When removing a bumper, you may need to use some spray lubricant, a long breaker bar, and an impact wrench

The lower portion of the fender between the wheel opening and the door was pushed back more than at the top. This, in turn, pushed the door back at the bottom, causing the door to essentially rotate clockwise.

The rotation at the front end displaced the rear part of the door outward. To properly align the door, the lower hinge will require work to move it back into the correct position. When the hinge has been reworked, the door will fit and operate properly.

to loosen the mounting hardware. Since the bumper hardware is usually exposed to the elements, it is among the first to corrode and rust. Use a floor jack or enlist the aid of a helper to support the bumper as your remove the last bolts and set it aside. After the bumper bolts are removed, verify that none of the bolts are bent, stripped, or otherwise damaged. If they are, replace them before you reinstall the repaired or replacement bumper.

Bumper Brackets

After the bumper has been removed, verify that the bumper brackets are not damaged and that the hardware securing them to the vehicle's chassis is still tight. If any of the brackets are damaged, they will need to be straightened or replaced, and then remounted to the vehicle. You should also verify that no mounting bolts have been sheared off. If they have, they will require replacement. You, with a helper if necessary, will need to drill out the broken portion to ensure that the bumper is properly secured later.

Bumper Repair

Any straightening method will most likely damage the chrome plating. So, you can hammer on the bumper in an effort to straighten it out and then have it re-chromed. Since the bumper is usually some pretty heavy-duty metal, it isn't as easy to straighten as body grade sheet metal. Additionally, if the bumper is to be re-chromed, no conven-

tional body filler can be used, as it would not withstand the temperature reached during the chroming process.

Even though you can do chrome plating at home, as discussed in my book *How to Plate, Polish and Chrome*, having a tank large enough for a bumper usually is not feasible for the hobbyist. Re-chroming a bumper that has been damaged will probably cost more than buying a new bumper. By the time you figure in time spent straightening and cost for re-chroming, buying a replacement bumper will most likely be more practical.

If the bumper is painted, rather than plated, you can do a certain amount of bodywork on it, just as if it were another piece of sheet metal. Again, it is going to require a bigger hammer as it is heavier material, but you can use body filler to smooth the surface before priming and painting.

Bumper Replacement

Whether the bumper is a replacement or has been refinished, reassembly is straightforward. Enlist an assistant to help you set the bumper into position and insert all of the bolts through the bumper and bumper brackets. Install a large washer over each bolt after it has passed through the bumper bracket, and then install a lock washer and nut, or a self locking nut. Hand-tighten the nuts and then verify that the bumper is centered side to side and sits level with the vehicle. When the bumper is positioned correctly, tighten all of the nuts with an appropriate sized wrench or socket.

CHAPTER 6
COLLISION REPAIR—
COMPOSITES

A great many different kinds of plastics are in use today on all types of automobile parts and assemblies. They range from acrylonitrile butadiene styrene (ABS) to ThermoPlastic Olefin (TPO) and sheet molded compounds (SMC) to reaction injection molded (RIM) plastic. Each has its own place, from rigid grille-work sections to flexible bumper covers.

This use of plastics (composites) in automobiles has changed the auto body repair business substantially. On the positive side, composites don't rust and are generally lighter weight than similar panels made of sheet metal.

These are two distinct advantages for the automobile manufacturers, as they indirectly have a positive effect on their sales: composites don't rust and lighter vehicles don't burn as much fuel. Eliminating rust and increasing corporate fuel averages is big business.

On the negative side, plastic-based composites, by their chemical makeup, are either brittle or flexible. Brittle composites, such as those used in many fenders, quarter panels, and door skins, will crack and break on impact. Flexible composites, such as those used in bumper/fascia assemblies, will withstand a certain amount

Contemporary bumpers are considerably different from those "5-mile-per-hour bumpers" on the 1980s and 1990s vehicles and are significantly different from bumpers of vehicles that are even older. The former typically had a tube in a tube arrangement of attaching the bumper to the vehicle's chassis, while the latter had formed metal brackets bolted to the bumper and the chassis. The white portion of this bumper is actually a piece of molded foam that covers a piece of alloy tubing, which spans across the front of the vehicle and is hidden when the bumper/fascia is in place.

Today's flexible bumper/fascia assemblies typically slide into grooves, tracks, or clips on the fender for alignment purposes. The bumper/fascia is then secured to the fender with a number of screws or bolts that are usually installed from the inside of the wheelwell, which virtually eliminates all fasteners from view.

of impact, but will not rebound once they are pushed beyond their elastic range.

Overall, newer vehicles are designed for the composite body panels to absorb most of the impact forces that occur in a collision. The substructure of these vehicles also absorbs shock throughout the vehicle's crumple zones. All in all, these design changes provide greater occupant safety in a collision, which is beyond a doubt a good thing. However, the vehicle involved in what seemed like a minor accident that you walked away from, may now be totaled out, or at least damaged beyond simple repair by the hobbyist body worker. Still, there are some repairs to these composite panels that you can undertake.

BASIC CRACK REPAIR

Whether the damaged composite panel is rigid or flexible, it is susceptible to cracks upon impact. As long as the affected panel is still partially connected or can be clamped back together in the correct shape, you can repair rather easily by using panel adhesive designed for composite au-

tomobile panels. Removing the panel to gain better access to the back side will be beneficial.

You should first clean the back of the panel with wax and grease remover to prevent contaminants from being trapped beneath panel adhesive. Then use a small grinder to scuff up the surface to promote adhesion. You should also use the grinder to cut a slight "V" groove along the crack to provide more surface area to which the adhesive can adhere. Cut a piece of 3M Duramix structural gauze to a size that will cover the crack to be filled. Then saturate the structural gauze with 3M Duramix adhesive (generically known as panel bond or panel adhesive). Then press the gauze into place, using a body filler spreader to work out any bubbles. After the adhesive becomes tacky, apply another piece of saturated structural gauze to increase the strength.

After the crack is patched from the back side and the panel adhesive dry to the touch, cosmetic repair to the outside can be completed. Use 36-grit sandpaper by hand or on a sanding disc to scuff the outside surface and then clean it with wax and grease remover. Mix an appropriate

To align the bumper/fascia assembly on the vehicle, the two notches shown near the top edge (toward upper left of photo) slide onto mating buttons on the fender. Bolts, screws, or other types of fasteners pass through the lower fender extension and into the mounting flange shown at the far left of the photo. Most likely, another fastener is used at the protrusion located on the top edge adjacent to the headlight or taillight. Yes, this is a front assembly, but the rear would attach in similar fashion.

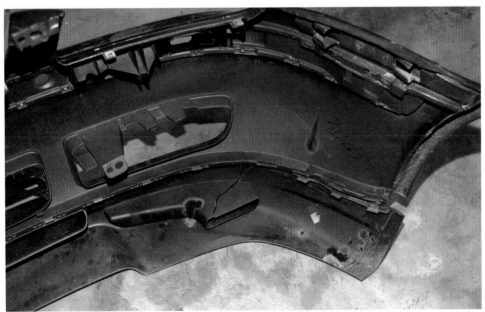

This panel was replaced rather than repaired; however, it could have been repaired if desired. Other than cosmetic damage that could have been easily repaired, some structural damage would have needed to be repaired as well. In the bodyline located about a third of the way up from the bottom, the bumper/fascia has a crack or tear that runs partially around a curve and then down across the air duct. By clamping the separated pieces back together and then applying 3M Duramix urethane adhesive and Duramix structural gauze, the assembly could be repaired.

amount of plastic body filler and hardener, and then use a spreader to press the filler into the crack and onto the surrounding area. As the filler begins to get tacky, begin sanding it with 80- or 100-grit sandpaper to remove the excess filler and then smooth it with 180- or 220-grit sandpaper. Apply additional filler if necessary and sand as required to match the surrounding surface in both shape and texture.

PANEL REPAIR/REPLACEMENT

If the damage goes beyond one crack, it can still be repaired as long as you can piece it together adequately to recre-ate the original shape and have access to the panel's back side. The repair will require panel adhesive and structural gauze. The procedure is fundamentally the same as for fixing a crack, as described previously. The major difference is that you may be required to use cardboard or masking tape to form up the front side of the surface that is being repaired; this will prevent the panel adhesive from passing through from the back and producing a high spot. When the original damaged panel is repaired or a replacement panel is prepped for paint, it can be reinstalled on the vehicle and painted using conventional paint procedures.

REPAIRING A BUMPER/FASCIA ASSEMBLY

The composite materials and wraparound design of the bumper/fascia assembly on contemporary vehicles absorb much of the force in a front end or rear end automobile accident. This means less damage to the main passenger compartment sheet metal and far less injuries to occupants.

Sometimes the bumper cover will sustain only minor damage like a crack or tear. In that event, you can save some money by repairing the damage and reusing the cover, rather than buying a new replacement piece. (Note that the cover is purely cosmetic. If the rigid crosspiece that lies beneath the cover and bolts to the car is damaged, it must be replaced regardless of whether you repair or replace the cover.) Follow along as we repair the fascia on a Chevrolet Cavalier.

A front impact chipped the paint on this Chevrolet Cavalier's front fascia and cracked the surrounding area. The impact also tore the flatter portion of the fascia. The good thing is that this damage can be repaired easily.

This is what the back side of the damaged areas looks like before any work is done (other than removing the damaged fascia from the vehicle).

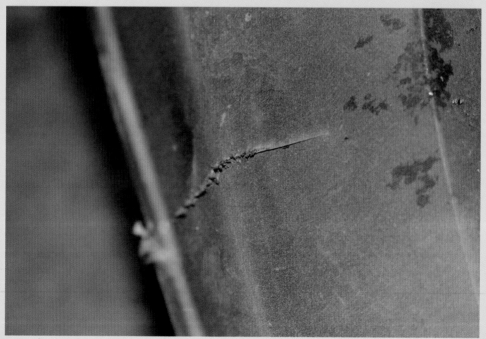

The first step is to clean the affected area with wax and grease remover so that no contaminants that would have a detrimental effect on the repair are pushed into the composite material or otherwise trapped by filler or paint. Spray or wipe the wax and grease remover on and then wipe it off with a clean paper towel.

Use a small grinder with a 36-50–grit disc to scuff up the back side of the fascia. Be careful that you don't build up too much heat or the composite material may start melting, balling up, and in general causing more work for you. The surface just needs to be scuffed a bit to give the structural gauze something rough to adhere to.

This is what the back side looks like when it has been scuffed properly and you are ready to apply the structural gauze to the area.

Prior to making the repair on the back side, go ahead and remove the paint in the immediate area of the repair on the front side as well. (You'll need to do more front-side sanding later so that the necessary layers of fillers can be feathered to match the existing contours.)

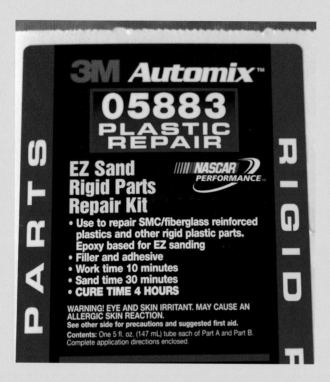

For this 3M Automix Plastic Repair kit, working time is 10 minutes from the time the two components are mixed. It can be sanded after 30 minutes, and is fully cured in four hours. At less than 30 dollars for the kit, it is affordable and easy enough to repair composite panels.

The kit consists of two components that are mixed in equal parts. When using these components, be sure to allow for plenty of ventilation as the odor is quite unpleasant.

Just as with body filler, squeeze the appropriate amount of the two components onto a mixing board, and then mix thoroughly by folding the materials onto each other repeatedly with a plastic spreader.

When there are no streaks of color in the mix, the adhesive is ready to apply.

Cut a piece of structural gauze to the necessary size to cover the damaged area. Using a plastic spreader, apply the adhesive over the damage, and then spread the structural gauze onto the adhesive with a plastic spreader. If the broken panel has any tendency toward misalignment, use a clamp (such as this spring clamp) to hold the two sides of the damage in proper position while the repair cures.

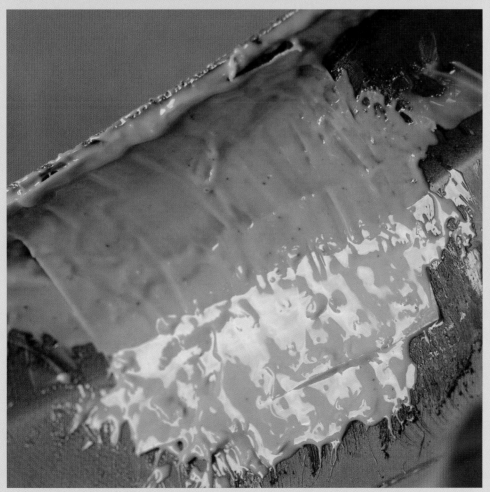

After the adhesive becomes tacky, mix some more of the two-part adhesive and spread that over the structural gauze to increase the strength of the repair. If you want, you can sand this area smooth after it cures, but since it is on the back side, I'm not going to bother. It only has to be level enough to sit flush over the foam padding underneath.

Right: *A bit of the adhesive has seeped through to the front side, so I smoothed that down with some 36-grit sandpaper on a rubber sanding block.*

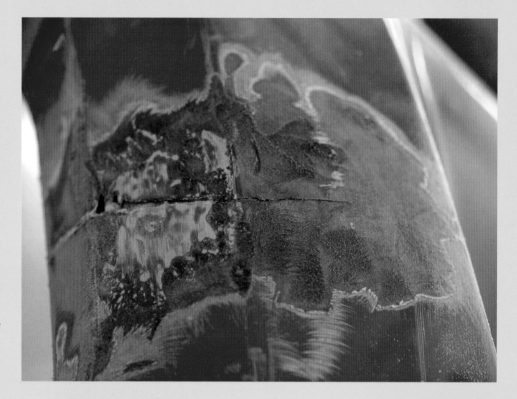

Below: *After mixing another batch of adhesive, I used a plastic spreader to spread the adhesive/ filler onto the front side of the bumper cover.*

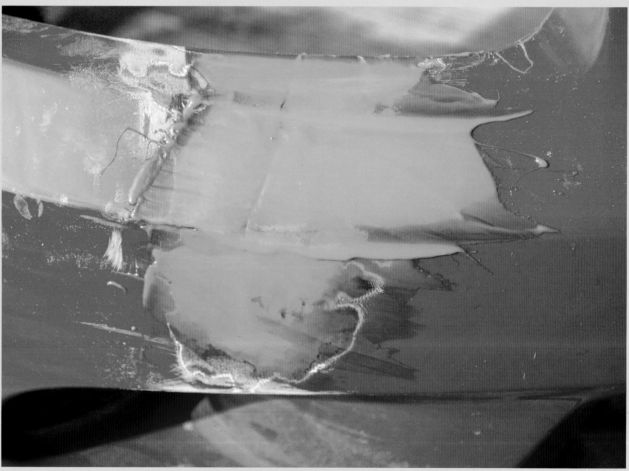

Above: *After giving it plenty of time to cure, I began block sanding the front side with a rubber sanding block and 36-grit sandpaper. I might have been able to use 80-grit sandpaper if I had not let the adhesive/filler cure quite as long.*

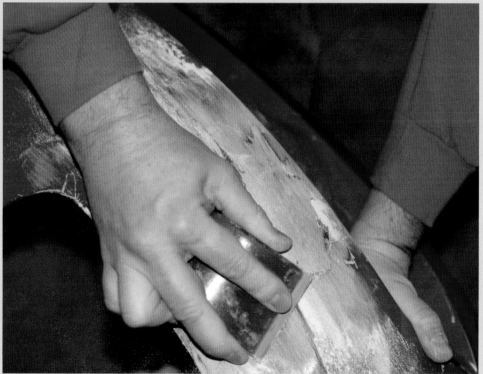

Left: *Still, after allowing the adhesive/filler to cure overnight, it only took about 30 minutes to get it sanded down.*

Right: *To increase the adhesion of the surface for the next batch of filler, be sure to sand beyond the limits of the adhesive/filler.*

Below: *After the sanding is completed, use compressed air and an air nozzle to blow away the dust, and then clean the area with wax and grease remover.*

Above: *Now mix a small amount of plastic body filler for a skim coat over the repair. Using a plastic spreader, spread this as smooth as you can.*

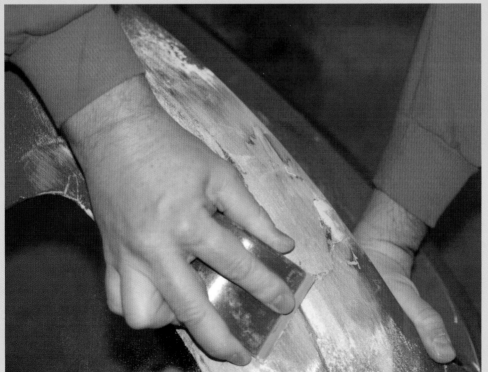

Left: *After waiting for the body filler to cure, begin sanding it with a sanding block wrapped with 80-grit sandpaper. By this time the bumper cover is beginning to look pretty good.*

97

Above: *It is difficult to see in the filler area, but if you look closely, you can see evidence of sanding in a cross-hatch pattern on the painted area. At this point, you would apply more filler if low spots are evident, or apply a guide coat of rattle can spray enamel and then do more block sanding.*

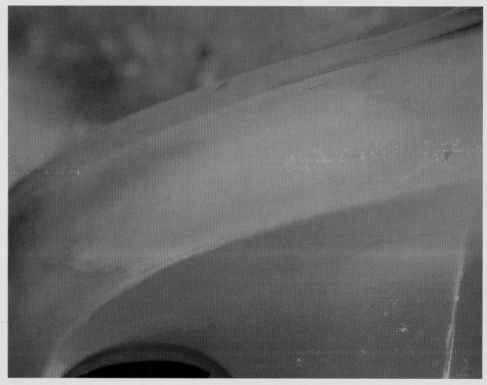

Right: *No more filler was necessary, so I applied two coats of primer/surfacer. This and the rest of the bumper cover would need to be block sanded, and then a sealer applied prior to paint.*

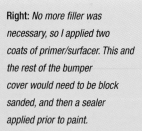

98

This late model GM pickup is typical of the many vehicles where glass is glued in place. Should the glass require removal, a small hole has to be cut in the butyl material that holds it in place. A cable is then inserted through this hole and handles are attached to each end of the cable. A person on the outside of the vehicle and another on the inside work together to pull the cable back and forth to cut the butyl.

An older GM truck provides an example of rubber molding securing the back glass. With the proper tool, this type of glass can be removed easily by one person, although two people are required to reinstall it.

GLASS REPLACEMENT

If you are merely repainting a vehicle or a portion thereof, it is not necessary to remove the window glass, as long as you can mask it properly. However, when faced with collision repair, it will often be necessary to remove the glass for a variety of reasons, the main reason being that it is cracked or broken. Even if the glass is not damaged, it may be easier to remove it and reinstall it later than to risk breaking it yourself during the repair process, depending on the piece involved. Since door glass is typically easy to remove and replace, you would be better off removing that glass than taking the chance of hitting it with a hammer and having to spend extra to replace it. Front windshield or rear glass is more difficult for the amateur to remove because it is held in place with adhesive and is physically larger. The pros make this look easy, but they know several tricks.

Since paint should be cured by the time you begin installing glass, consider laying strips of wide automotive masking tape—not generic tape that might leave adhesive residue on surfaces—along window frame edges. This will help guard against accidental bumps that could cause paint scratches or nicks; even so installing glass after a vehicle body has been painted must be done with care in order to avoid this. Even the smallest paint chip could allow an oxidation process to begin. Once started, especially in areas hidden by trim, oxidation will spread under layers of paint and not be noticed until severe rust damage causes

This illustration shows the three major steps of installing a glass that is held in place by rubber molding. The rubber molding is first installed on the glass, then a rope is inserted in the groove of the molding that fits over the pinch weld in the window area. The rubber molding is then fit over the pinch weld, the rope is pulled out slowly from inside the vehicle, while slight pressure is applied from the outside, just ahead of the rope. When the rope is pulled out, the rubber molding is left hugging the pinch weld and the glass is secured in place.

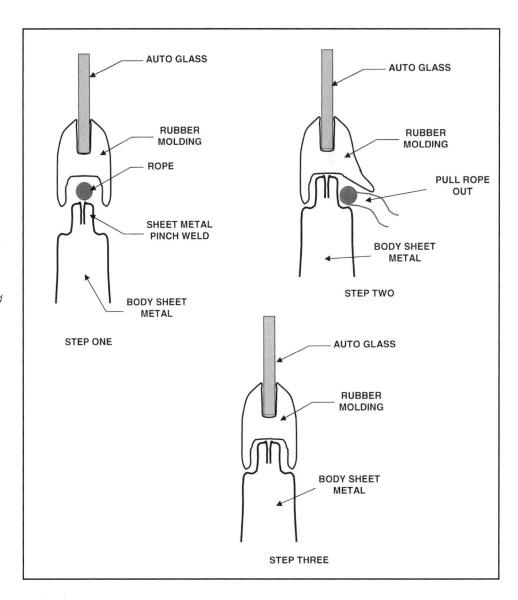

paint finishes to bubble or crack. Should that occur, repair efforts could require extensive metalwork and new paint.

Along with recognizing the importance of preventing paint chips while installing glass, you should be concerned about watertight seals all around the window perimeters. Not only are water leaks annoying, but they can also lead to corrosion damage on metal panels and rot or mildew in upholstery and carpeting.

Window glass is held in place by different means. Not all makes and models utilize identical attachment methods. Some may feature clips, others might rely on thick rubber molding, and many call for strips of butyl- or urethane-based sealers to hold panels safely in place. If you are not familiar with auto glass installation, you may consider hiring a professional to complete the work for you. Most auto glass businesses offer mobile service, sending specialists to

complete glass installations, or removals, at your working location.

Installation of fixed-glass units with urethane sealer actually adds a degree of structural strength to some automobiles. Windshields and side-mounted fixed-glass units on newer cars and vans are commonly secured in place by continuous beads of urethane sealer. In some cases, a bead of butyl material is used instead of urethane. Butyl has a strength of approximately 5 psi, while urethane boasts an adhesion strength of approximately 500 psi.

Instances that call for butyl beads alone are usually those where extensive bodywork was completed at, or near, window openings. If you are concerned about possible imperfect body window openings and resultant water leaks, you may need glass removal so body sheet-metal adjustments can be made. Since butyl is not nearly as strong as urethane, removing these glass units is much easier.

About the only way to remove fixed-glass units secured by butyl or urethane beads is to cut through the beads with a special tool. Essentially, the tool consists of a piece of strong wire with handles at each end and requires two people to operate. Make an opening in the urethane bead and insert the wire through it. With handles then attached at both ends, a person on the inside and another on the outside maneuver the wire around fixed glass to cut through the urethane bead. Afterward, use a special solvent to loosen old bead material for its removal.

The installation of fixed-glass units requires their supportive body opening be clean of all contaminants. Then, lay a bead of butyl material around the window opening perimeter. For butyl-only installations, make sure the bead is solidly shaped. If you will be using urethane as well, angle the butyl bead's side that touches the vehicle body at about 45 degrees. Along that angle, place the urethane material to fill in the triangular void left open by the butyl bead's 45-degree angle.

For either kind of installation, butyl actually holds glass in place. This is an important factor for urethane jobs, as it takes some time for that material to fully cure. While it is curing, butyl holds glass in a fixed position. The end result should be a near-perfect and leak-free installation.

The tools and materials needed to remove and install fixed-glass units are available at auto body paint and supply stores. Be sure you fully understand all installation instructions for the products that you use. In addition, have a helper available to assist you in removing or replacing glass units, as they can be quite heavy and cumbersome.

Replacing a Fixed Window

There are basically two types of windows in an automobile, fixed glass and opening glass. Fixed glass is installed where the windows do not open, such as the windshield, back window, and rear quarter windows. Glass from fixed windows is detached by first removing any trim around the window seal and the rubber weather stripping by using a special tool designed just for this task, and then pushing the window glass outward. Any residual window caulk or sealant must be removed from the sheet metal around the window opening. Some of these windows are glued in place, while others are held in place by rubber weather stripping. For the former type, the sheet-metal window opening must be clean and free of debris, broken glass, and contaminants. Clean the area with wax and grease remover, and then apply the glue to the flange in the window opening. Set the glass into position and press it into place to

ensure full contact with the glue. The vehicle must remain still for the amount of time required for the glue to set.

To install glass that is secured by rubber molding, you will need a piece of $3/8$-inch rope and an assistant. The rope should be made of nylon or other material that will slide easily and will need to be long enough to wrap around the perimeter of the glass being installed with a foot or two of overlap. Begin by cleaning the sheet metal where the glass sits in place, making sure that any debris or rust is gone. Fit the rubber molding around the glass, making sure that it is correctly oriented (i.e. the corners of the rubber molding are at the corners of the glass, the top is at the top, etc.). Place the rope in the groove of the molding that is designed to fit onto the pinch weld of the body's sheet metal. The middle of the rope should be positioned near the middle top of the windshield and wrapped all around the rubber molding so that both ends of the rope overlap near the middle of the bottom of the windshield. Make sure that the rope stays within this groove and then lubricate the rubber molding with soapy water, glass cleaner, or other lubricant. Avoid silicone spray as it can create fish eyes in any paint you apply to the vehicle afterward.

With the help of an assistant, place the glass with rubber molding on the opening of the vehicle, from the outside. Verify that the glass is located properly. Make sure that the loose ends of rope are located inside the vehicle and are not caught between the glass and the sheet-metal body. As one person slowly pulls the rope away from the glass, the other person applies slight, but even pressure to the glass from the outside, just ahead of the rope. This will cause the rubber molding to slip over the pinch weld in the window opening. Work your way all around the glass until the entire rope has been pulled out. In the corners of the glass or anywhere else where the rope is difficult to pull out, apply a little less pressure on the glass. Make sure that none of the rubber molding is folded over on itself and that it is laying flat. Clean off any excess lubricant and you are done.

Replacing an Opening Window

Opening glass includes windows that are rolled down manually or electrically, or the foldout type in vans and extended cab pickup trucks. In either case, the glass to be replaced is removed from the roll-up track located at the bottom or the hinged mounting point that is usually at the front of the glass. Surprisingly, opening glass is typically easier for the first-time installer than fixed glass; however, the specific procedure will vary somewhat depending on the vehicle.

REINSTALLING WEATHER STRIPPING AND DOOR GLASS

Any time when a door is damaged, the glass and interior door panel will need to be removed to make the necessary repairs. The key to carrying out this task is finding out how the interior door panel is secured. Very often on newer vehicles, the door panel simply snaps into place, and therefore can be pried off. However, there will usually be one or a few screws that are located around the interior door latch mechanism, such as inside the door pull and other "out of view" locations. With the interior door panel removed, you will now have access to the various bolts and screws that hold everything in place inside the door. When disassembling the door, make sure that you gather and save all hardware and document how things fit together for reassembly with notes and photos.

Reassembling the door, its glass, and weather stripping is typically the reverse of disassembly. Follow along as Mike at Jerry's Auto Body reinstalls these items on an SUV that has both fixed and opening glass in one door.

There will be a piece of rubber weather stripping that fits between the glass and all portions of the window frame where there needs to be a weather-tight seal. This particular door requires two pieces since there are actually two pieces of glass. In this instance, a tall, skinny piece of glass is fixed in place, with a division bar adjacent to the front edge to provide a track for the opening section.

If you are not sure how some of the pieces fit into place, refer to the other side of the vehicle if it is not damaged. If both sides are damaged and therefore require disassembly, you may need to refer to the photos or notes that you took upon disassembly.

Left: *Since this weather stripping is made especially for this vehicle, the corners are molded in and therefore provide a hint as to how it fits into place. If you were using "universal" weather stripping, this would not be so evident. Regardless of universal or model specific, the weather stripping is pushed into the opening around the perimeter of the window opening.*

Below: *There may be notches in the door sheet metal that provide indications of proper alignment of the weather stripping. Just make sure that you get it aligned and seated properly to avoid leaks.*

Since this Jeep has two pieces of glass in the door, along with a division bar, the operable glass is installed first. Installing the glass can be tricky, but the main thing to remember is to not get it in a bind, which would cause it to crack or break. Door glass will often have some slight curve to it, which will often necessitate installing the glass from the outside, as shown, or it may need to be slid in at an angle.

Right: *By looking through the access panel, you can align the bottom of the glass with its window track and riser mechanism. There will usually be some clips, rather than nuts and bolts, to secure the glass to the riser. However the glass is held, make sure that it is secure but not over-tightened.*

Below left: *With the door glass installed, you should install the window crank mechanism, or connect the power window switch, and slowly run the glass through its up and down cycle a couple of times. If there is any binding, stop and correct the situation.*

Below right: *Now the fixed glass and its attached division bar can be installed. As seen in this photo, the division bar is much longer than the glass, as it also serves as a track for the glass that moves. Carefully insert the division bar into the door opening and continue sliding it downward until it is in position. Be careful to not catch any wires or door latch linkages.*

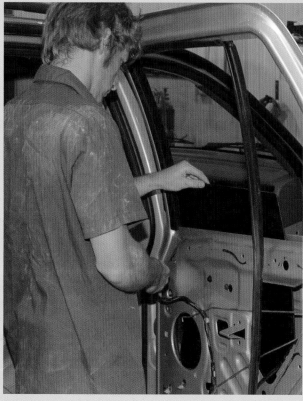

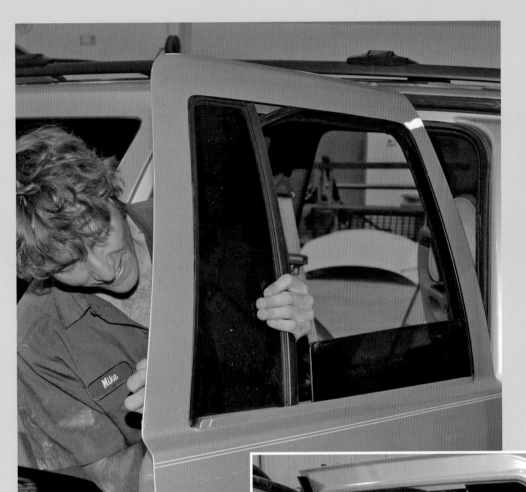

Do not use a hammer, but you may need to "bump" the division bar with your hand once or twice to fully seat it in the opening.

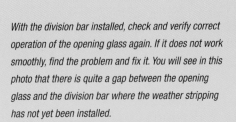

With the division bar installed, check and verify correct operation of the opening glass again. If it does not work smoothly, find the problem and fix it. You will see in this photo that there is quite a gap between the opening glass and the division bar where the weather stripping has not yet been installed.

Almost forgot to install a screw at the top of the division bar. Pull the weather stripping down as required and install the screw.

Insert the loose end of the weather stripping into the door opening. Now press the weather stripping into place around the top of the window opening and along the front edge of the division bar.

The division bar will usually be secured to the door by one or two screws. Do not forget to install them.

This particular vehicle secures the division bar at a total of three places. One is at the top of the window opening, the second is just below the bottom of the window opening, and the third is near the bottom of the division bar. Making sure that the division bar is secure will help to ensure that there is no binding in the operation of the window.

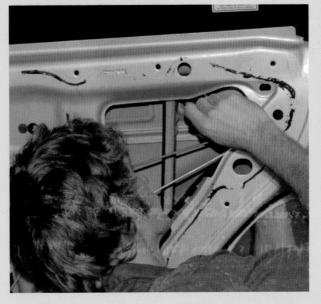

The exterior door handle is now installed and secured to the door. On this vehicle, it is secured with two bolts that pass through the interior of the door and thread into the handle mechanism.

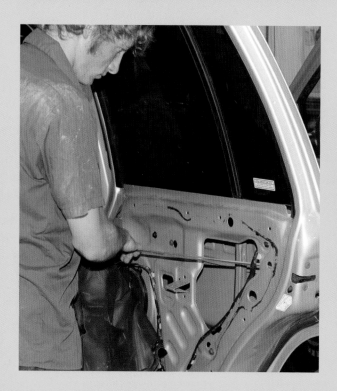

The actuator rod(s) must now be reconnected between the exterior door handle, the interior door handle, and the latch mechanism. You may need to refer to your photos and notes taken during disassembly to make sure you install this correctly.

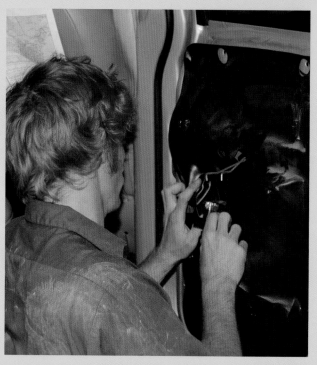

Some vehicles have a flexible panel that snaps into place between the door and the interior door panel. This is basically a method of insulation/sound deadening. If your vehicle has one, reinstall it and any stereo speakers fitted in the door.

If your vehicle has power door locks/windows, install the switch in the interior door panel from the back side. You will find that another couple of inches of wire for these power accessories will be helpful. Now reinstall the interior door panel. It may snap in place or be secured with small screws.

Now carefully install the exterior trim that is designed to prevent rainwater and other moisture from running down the door glass and inside of the door panel.

You may need to apply some extra effort to seat the trim in place, but be sure that it is aligned properly beforehand. A few taps with your fist will usually do it if the panel is aligned properly.

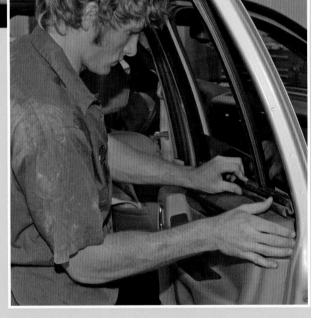

Above: *Install the interior garnish molding at the bottom of the window. On newer vehicles it will generally snap into place, but on older vehicles it might be secured with trim screws.*

Left: *In addition to the snaps that secure this interior door panel in place, one screw "hidden" away in the door pull secures it.*

CHAPTER 7
RUST REPAIR

Obviously a collision is not the only thing that ruins automobiles; rust can be just as devastating. Anyplace where humidity meets unprotected sheet metal, rust is hard at work eating its way through it. Sadly, you may not even know rust is present, as it tends to do its damage to areas of your vehicle that you don't normally see during everyday operation. When dealing with rust, you will need to determine whether it is just surface rust, or if it is actually rust-through.

If it is mere surface rust with solid metal beneath it, you can sand it off and apply epoxy primer to protect the metal. If the rust is more severe, with either complete rust-through or severely pitted sheet metal, more extensive repairs are necessary before you can apply paint. This may necessitate media blasting or use of a chemical stripper, along with application of epoxy primer, followed by application of a high build primer-surfacer. It may be necessary to weld in patch panels if rust is severe enough.

It should be noted that primer-surfacer or even epoxy primer alone will not prevent rust from re-occurring. Proper application of paint to all metal surfaces, along with regular washing and applications of wax is the best defense. Until paint is used, an application of epoxy primer is the most effective rust deterrent. Simply applying primer-surfacer will not prevent rust, as it is actually porous and therefore soaks up moisture, which is the primary cause of rust.

The salmon (pink) color on this firewall and cowl is weld-through primer. The primer provides short-term protection to the metal surface, but does not have to be ground away prior to doing any welding. After any welding is completed and prior to applying any body filler, primer, or paint, you should apply epoxy primer.

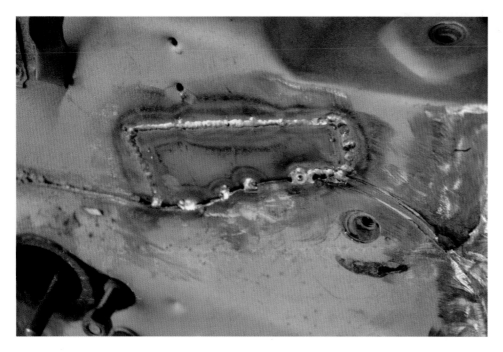

A small patch panel has been fabricated in the shop, and then welded in place to fill a stock opening in the firewall that will no longer be required. For this firewall or any flat areas, patch panels can easily be cut from 18-22–gauge sheet metal to fill any large holes.

Special care must be taken any time you are doing bodywork to a convertible, especially if the doors are going to be removed. Since there is no upper body support provided by a roof, the body tub can buckle at the door openings. The solution is to brace across the top of the door opening on each side.

Temporarily tack welding some angle iron or electrical conduit between the cowl and the rear quarter panels, front to back and between the quarter panels side to side, can minimize or eliminate damage due to body flex. The brace must be suitably strong in both compression and tension to prevent the opening from narrowing or widening as you raise and support the body.

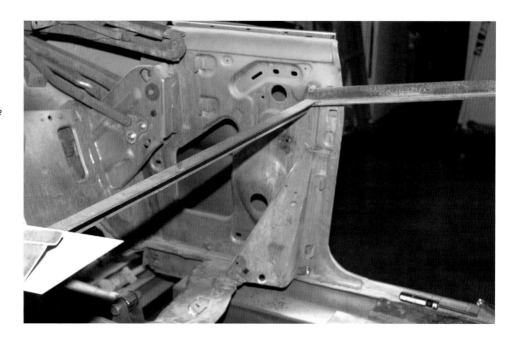

PATCH PANELS

Patch panels have been used extensively on vintage restorations and hot rods, but their use is becoming more common on later model vehicles as the average vehicle age grows older. Patch panels differ from replacement panels as they are just a portion of the entire panel. Common patch panels are used to repair lower doors, portions of fenders, rocker panels, or cab corners on pickup trucks.

An ever expanding restoration aftermarket is providing more patch panels for more vehicles every year. As more vehicles begin to show their rust prone areas, more companies begin producing parts to repair these areas. If a certain make and model of vehicle begins to show a trend of rusting on the left side of the trunk floor, the aftermarket will work to fill this demand. If, however, yours is the only one that rusts on the right side, the panel may not be available. The automotive aftermarket develops new products based largely on the laws of supply and demand. If you are working on a mainstream vehicle, chances are that the necessary patch panel for your particular application is available. Even if available patch panels are not large enough to cover the entire damaged area, one may be useful for repairing its intricate bodylines.

If the sheet metal has been media blasted, chemically dipped, or stripped by some other method, the extent of the necessary rust repair is fairly obvious. However, if the suspect panel still wears a coat of paint, you will need to do some investigating. If the paint is bubbling up, the panel is most likely rusty beneath the surface. You can use a small screwdriver or ice pick to map out the extent of the rust. Begin by poking either tool into the middle of the suspected area of rust. If it goes right through, you do have a rust-through problem and should continue poking in small circles and extending outward from the center. When you begin hitting metal where the screwdriver or ice pick will not go through, you are most likely hitting sheet metal that is still usable. However, there may be additional rust pockets located nearby.

After completing this probing to determine the extent of the rust, purchase a patch panel that will cover the entire area if possible. Not all patch panels will be large enough to cover all areas of rust. Prior to cutting away any of the area that will be removed, compare the patch panel with the area that is to be repaired. If possible, slip the panel roughly into place over the existing metal and trace around the edge with a permanent marker. This will show the limits of what you can remove, but you should not simply cut at this line as you will need some overlap to affix the patch. You should mark a second line approximately an inch inside of this line and use it to indicate the area to be removed.

Now use a plasma cutter, die grinder, reciprocating saw, or tin snips to cut along this second line to remove the rusty area. Prior to welding in any patch panels or replacement panels, you must verify that the vehicle is supported properly. If the vehicle's body is twisted in any way and a new panel is welded in place, it will cause major panel alignment problems later on. Fit the new panel into place and check it for proper alignment. Then clamp it into place and weld.

This lower door shows indications of prior damage that was repaired with body filler that was never completely sanded. It was also protected only with a coat or two of lacquer-based primer, which did not provide adequate protection from the elements, resulting in rust-through. Don't fall into this trap! Once you start the job, finish it. What could be more disheartening than watching the prep work you did rust away knowing that you need to redo it—and that you may have done more damage because of extra paint you removed when you started the job?

This is the opposite door of the same vehicle, with the same poor quality of repair. Although the rust-through is not as bad on this side, it could have been prevented completely by finishing the repair rather than just applying primer.

Which weld type to use is largely dependent upon the actual panel being replaced, the type of welder being used, and the welder's skills. When welding with a MIG welder, start with 1/8-inch tacks and skip around so the panel does not get too hot, as this will cause distortion. Another tip is to use your air hose with an air nozzle to blow cool air on the welds to keep them from getting too hot.

After you have completed all welding, you should clean the patched area with wax and grease remover, apply epoxy primer, and then perform finish bodywork to the surrounding area. Follow with primer-surfacer and block sanding as necessary prior to sealer and topcoats.

Rocker Panels

Rocker panels frequently rust out for a variety of reasons. They are located low on the car and therefore require a little extra effort to clean them when washing the vehicle. Moisture that seeps down the door glass and into the door often drains onto them, but never dries while the door is closed. Also, rocker panels are often made of folded sheet metal that overlaps the floor panel. This is usually sealed with seam sealer from the factory, but when that deteriorates, moisture and debris collect between the panels, causing rust.

Replacement rocker panels are available for most vehicles and are easy to install, requiring only a MIG welder.

REPLACING A PARTIAL QUARTER PANEL

To get the lowdown on installing a replacement quarter panel, I visited Morfab Customs where Brent Schmelz was working on an early Chevrolet Camaro. The original quarter panel had already been removed so that the new seam would be at the top bodyline where the quarter panel goes from horizontal to vertical. The original panel was cut away with a plasma cutter, but a reciprocating saw, die grinder, or sheet-metal shears could have been used. The replacement quarter from Goodmark Industries was aligned and clamped into place at the tail panel, at the front of the panel at the door, and where the wheelwell aligns with the wheelhouse. Using a MIG welder, the new quarter panel was spot welded approximately every 6 inches and then seam welded for the entire length of the mating seam.

This is actually a different vehicle than the one in the following photos, but it is the same make and model and will be treated to the same panel replacement. For this particular vehicle, the replacement panel is designed to be welded on precisely at the bodyline that delineates the profile of the rear quarter panel.

After removing the original quarter panel, any loose crumbs of rust were removed from the inner structure. To prevent further formation of rust, two coats of POR-15 have been applied. The POR-15 is not a product that should be used as a topcoat; however, it is designed to "paint over rust" to help protect areas that never received any protective coating from the factory.

When installing the quarter panel, it should be stitch welded around the perimeter. Note that the trapezoidal-shaped sheet-metal panel above the wheelhouse should be plug welded to the top of the wheelhouse. Either this vehicle has been repaired incorrectly before, or the welding was not completed at the factory. Evidence such as this should be a clue that you should double-check everything when aligning panels, as some things may not be correct.

Above: The original quarter panel has been removed and the replacement panel installed. It was aligned, tack welded in place, double-checked to verify proper alignment, and then stitch welded along the entire seam.

Left: The light gray area is the portion of the replacement quarter panel that has been scuffed up prior to welding, while the black area is the primer that was applied to the replacement panel by the manufacturer. With the high quality of the stitch welds securing the quarter panel in place, the weld itself is difficult to see, even from a short distance.

Still, the welds should be ground down so that they are flush with the body or slightly below. By using an angle head die grinder and a 36-grit disc, Brent makes reasonably quick work of this.

Any time you are using a grinder, please wear eye protection to save your eyesight. Brent should be wearing long sleeves and a face mask, but first-degree skin burns are not permanent.

As Brent completes the grinding, the basic location of the weld becomes more evident, as shown in the photo, although evidence of the weld virtually disappears. Grinding the weld smooth will eliminate any minor pinholes that could come back to haunt you later.

You must take the time to grind the welds in the intricate areas as well. Bodywork involves layers of tasks, so each one must be completed as accurately and completely as possible, or it will have a negative impact on tasks that follow.

Above: *After an initial pass, Brent checks to verify that he did not miss any welds. Finding some that are still a little high, he hits them with a grinder again.*

Right: *From this perspective, you can gain a better idea of where the partial quarter panel is attached to the body, along with how much area should be ground smooth.*

Even though this is a new replacement panel it is not perfect, therefore it will need a skim coat of filler. For the filler to adhere properly, a DA orbital sander with 80- to 100-grit sandpaper is used to scuff the surface.

Fiberglass-reinforced body filler should always be used as the first filler over areas that have been welded, such as replacement or patch panels, as it greatly improves adhesion of additional materials. It is also highly recommended for areas that are rust prone.

A plastic cutting board, such as one that would be used in the kitchen, makes a perfect surface for mixing body filler. They are inexpensive, very durable, and are easy to clean up. On whatever you use as a palette, pour or scoop the desired amount of filler onto the middle of it.

Squeeze the recommended amount of hardener onto the filler. You will gain a sense of how much to apply as you progress through the project, but it will be a trial-and-error process when you first begin. Typically, a proportionate amount of hardener is used with the filler (in other words, one quarter of the hardener should be used with one quarter of the filler).

Using a plastic spreader, fold the filler onto itself and into the ribbon of hardener.

Continue this folding-over motion from each side until the filler and hardener are thoroughly mixed, which is when the two are one consistent color and there are no streaks.

Above: *Using a clean spreader (the largest size that will fit into the area being filled), spread the filler onto the surface to be filled. Spread the filler so that it is not more than ⅛ inch thick in any spot.*

Left: *The purpose of this fiberglass reinforced filler is to encase and protect the weld from the elements that might cause rust to develop at some later time. Apply the filler directly over the weld and to each side about 2 to 3 inches.*

Apply the filler to the seam in the more confined areas as well.

Much of this filler will be sanded off, but a little precision now will spare you sanding time later.

Again, make sure that the entire welded area is covered to provide the best protection against formation of rust.

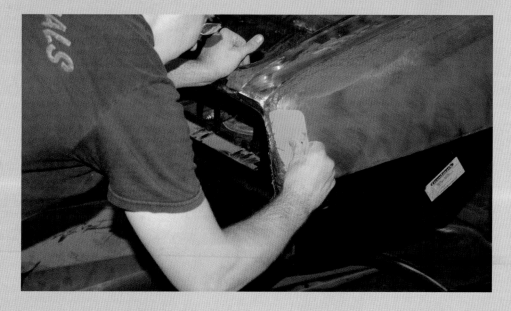

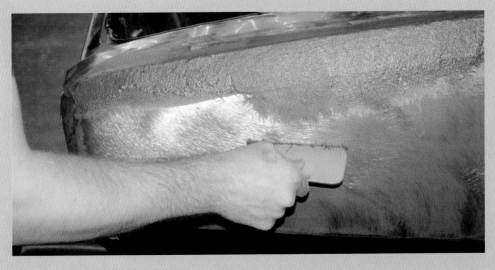

Left: *Although you can sand it off later, you can scrape off any excess filler with less effort before it begins to set.*

Below: *In this photo, you can see that fiberglass reinforced filler has been applied along the entire weld and extends down onto the quarter panel about 3 inches. This 3-inch overlap provides room to feather out the filler by sanding it smooth with the adjacent areas.*

RUST REPAIR

You can use 80- or 100-grit sandpaper to smooth the fiberglass reinforced filler, but a cheese grater file works better and faster. Some of these files are flat, while others have a rounded shape and seem to be more durable and less likely to break.

The filler requires a few minutes to set, but you should begin sanding or filing before it sets completely. When it is at the right consistency, the filler will come off in strips just as cheese would come through a cheese grater.

When using a cheese grater file, you are just concerned with taking the rough edges or high spots off the filler. It is much smoother than originally, but still requires lots of block sanding to get the sort of excellent invisible repair you are after.

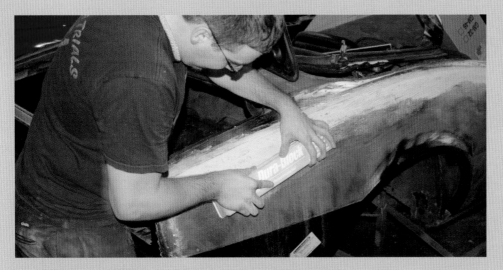

With the high spots knocked off, break out your favorite long board sanding block and some 80- to 100-grit sandpaper. Sand all of the fiberglass reinforced filler until it is smooth.

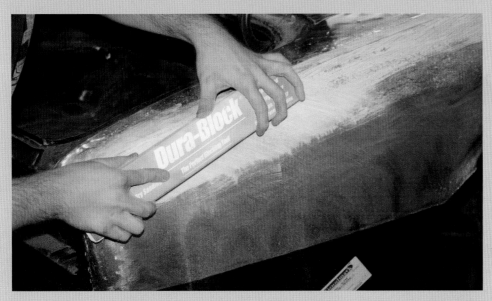

By using the longest sanding block that will fit in the area, you will be working toward getting the area flat (not wavy), as well as smooth. More filler will cover this layer, but the sooner you get the filler flat, the better.

The extra effort to apply the fiberglass reinforced filler will go a long way toward preventing rust in the weld area, where primer was sanded off of the replacement panel.

Right: *Unless you are a true metal craftsperson, you will most likely need to use at least a little bit of filler to get the replacement panel suitable for painting. Starting with no more than 1/8 inch of filler and then sanding most of it off, you will end up with merely a skim coat when you are finished. It does however provide enough material thickness to sand the body panels perfectly smooth and flat.*

Below: *After mixing the body filler as described previously, you are ready to apply it with a spreader. This filler will completely cover the fiberglass reinforced filler applied previously and will serve as a transition between that substrate and the areas that do not have any filler.*

RUST REPAIR

First spread all of the mixed filler on the area to be filled.

Then go back with a plastic spreader and smooth out the filler, eliminating ridges in the process. As you mix and use additional filler, you will no doubt learn to use more or less hardener based on how long it takes you to get it spread out and how long you have to wait before you can begin sanding it.

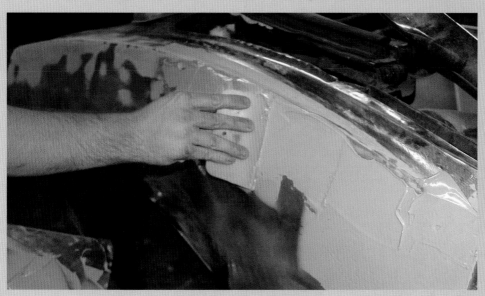

If you are going to be working a large area, you can mix the filler and hardener a little cooler so that you will have more time to finesse the filler prior to sanding. However, you do need to mix it stiff enough so that it does not fall off of vertical surfaces like quarter panels.

Although it takes some practice to figure out the correct amount, try to mix enough filler to cover the entire area within any one panel that you are working on at one time. This will help to eliminate low areas between applications and will allow you to "work" the entire area at one time.

When the entire area has begun to set up, you can begin scraping off high spots with a cheese grater file. If the file causes gouges in the filler, let it sit a while longer. If the filler begins peeling off as it goes through the grater, you are good to go. Working the filler at this consistency will be much easier than when it is fully cured.

After you have taken off the high spots with the cheese grater file, flatten and smooth the surface by using a sanding board with 100-grit sandpaper, then with 220-grit, and then with 400-grit.

Above: *To eliminate wavy panels, remember to move the sanding board or block back and forth in all directions. However, be careful around bodylines or other ridges so that you do not eliminate the crispness of the sheet-metal stamping.*

Left: *Occasionally, you should use an air hose with medium pressure to blow away any buildup of body filler from the sandpaper. Be sure to direct the air pressure away from you and anyone else in the area.*

129

REPLACING A FULL QUARTER PANEL

Keith Moritz and Brent Schmelz at Morfab Customs were also installing new full quarter panels on an early Chevrolet Nova. The basic procedure is the same as for a partial quarter panel, but in this instance, the sail panel for the hardtop comes into play.

This Nova is in better condition than some, but there is some rust in the rear quarter panels. The front fenders have already been replaced and a cowl induction hood installed. The doors are in pretty good shape, so they will be used.

RUST REPAIR

Most of the rust is located around the wheelwell, so a smaller patch panel could be installed. However, if you are paying the going labor rate to have this work done, it is probably not any more expensive to replace the full quarter panel. The dark spot across the sail panel is where the factory-installed lead has been burned away from the seam between the roof and the rear quarter panel.

At the factory, a fair amount of lead is used to fill and smooth seams where the vehicle designers do not want you to know there is a seam. Before any of these panels can be removed, the lead needs to be burned away with a torch. Be sure to wear a respirator when burning off lead, as it is a toxin. Wear proper gloves and eye protection when using a torch as well.

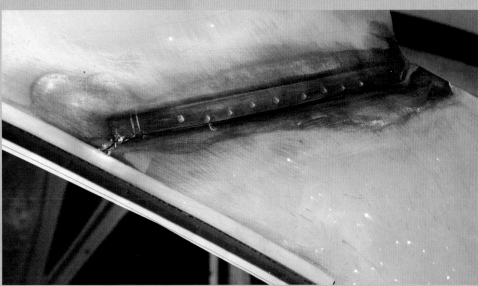

This is what the sail panel seam looks like after the lead has been melted away from where the roof and quarter panel meet. With the lead gone, you can see that the roof had a flanged panel that fit to the outside of the quarter panel and was then plug welded.

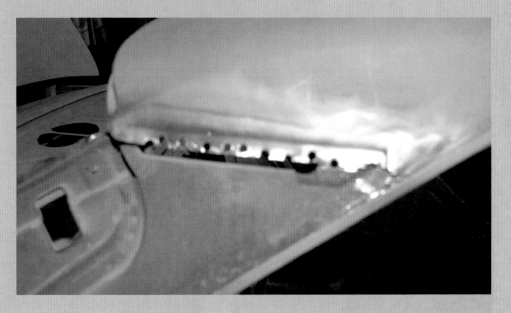

On the opposite side of the vehicle, the lead has been melted away and the original quarter panel removed. The replacement panel will need to slide up beneath this overlap.

Above: *The passenger-side quarter panel is slid into position for a test fit. At this point, the quarter sits a little higher than it should. Closer inspection reveals that the lower flange of the replacement quarter is not bent to quite the correct angle.*

Right: *Using a pair of duckbill pliers, Keith carefully folds the lower flange of the replacement quarter panel to the correct shape.*

A quarter panel never looks as big as it does when it is off the vehicle. Have an assistant help when you are fitting quarter panels. Brent (left) and Keith (right) carefully place the quarter panel into position.

After sliding the quarter panel beneath the roof edge, both of them check for proper alignment at their respective ends of the replacement panel.

133

Have plenty of clamps handy. Brent already has the quarter panel clamped into place at the top, but is checking to verify that the alignment at the tail pan is correct.

The gray area to the left of the clamp is where lead was melted out of the factory seam. You can see that the bodylines that will be exposed when the trunk is opened align quite nicely between the new and old panels.

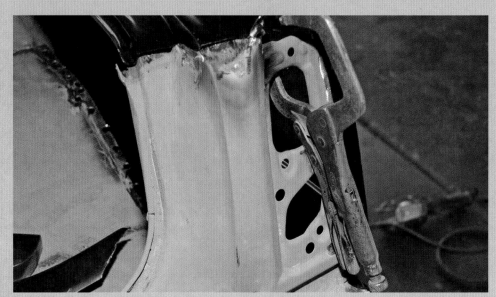

Initial reaction upon checking the fit is that the quarter panel is a little high at the door; however the quarter is aligned properly. Closer inspection reveals an uneven gap at the bottom of the door. By making a slight adjustment at the door hinges, this will raise the door at the back to align with the quarter panel and equalize the gap at the bottom of the door.

Above: *While Brent is removing the front fender to gain access to the door hinge, the quarter panel looks pretty good overall. Minor adjustments have yet to be made, but there is not any rust in the quarter panels anymore.*

Left: *By removing the front fender, you can gain access to the door hinges. Unless you are planning to remove the door completely, loosen the bolts securing the hinges just enough to move the door as desired. When you get the door into the right position, make sure that you retighten the bolts.*

While Keith checks the door alignment, Brent loosens or tightens the mounting bolts as needed.

With the quarter panel in place and aligned with the door, Brent installs some temporary self-tapping sheet-metal screws. The alignment is great at this point, but the opposite side quarter panel and a replacement tail pan still need to be installed, so it is too soon to weld anything in place.

Clamps will still hold the quarter panel at the back, but a few more temporary screws around the door opening will be installed to maintain the correct positioning. After the other replacement panels are installed, the quarter panel can be tack welded in place and the screws removed.

RUST REPAIR

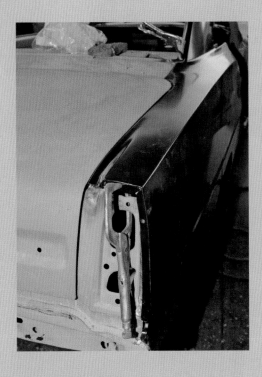

At the door, you should verify proper alignment between the quarter panel and the trunk lid. You will need to verify that the trunk lid is centered side to side and that it is the same height as both of the quarter panels.

After getting the quarter panel secured in place, simply sit back and give it a look from a distance. How do the bodylines line up? Now is the time to find and fix anything that looks amiss.

Take another look at an area where special attention needs to be taken to verify proper alignment. There are several vertical lines in this area where the full quarter panel should align with the original tail pan.

Since the center of the tail pan was solid and in good condition, the original center was left in place. The ends of the original tail pan were cut off and replaced with the end portions that were cut from the replacement tail pan.

Right: *At the taillight area of the tail pan, the quarter panel is plug welded into place. These welds should be ground down before any primer is applied.*

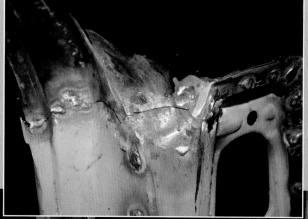

Below: *The driver side of the tail pan was not in quite as good condition as the passenger side, so more of the replacement panel has been used on that side.*

Right: *The driver-side replacement quarter panel is installed by following the same procedure as the passenger side. The only difference is the gas filler door, but that is negligible at this point.*

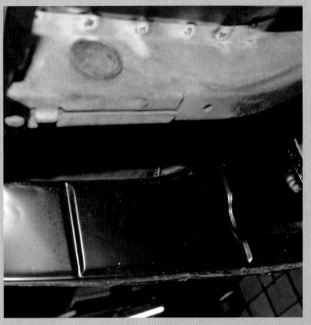

After installing the replacement quarter panel, the roof is secured to it with a group of plug welds across the top of the sail panel and down the flange of the rear window opening. These welds are then ground down, and the seam between the roof and the quarter panel is filled with body filler.

From beneath the car, this is a shot of the driver-side outer wheelhouse and trunk floor drop off. These pieces fill the gap between the inner wheelhouse and the inside of the quarter panel.

Whether doing collision repair or rust repair, a flourishing automotive aftermarket is making resurrection of many desirable cars feasible. So, do not be too quick to write off that older vehicle just because it is no longer in pristine condition.

This rocker panel/running board on a 1955 Chevy truck has various damage that will be repaired by installing a replacement panel. Essentially, this piece is folded sheet metal that has some overlap. The seam sealer, if even used at the factory, is long gone and rust has begun forming between the panels. Sometimes it is better to replace a panel than attempt to repair it.

The lower portion of this door jamb had some rust-through. With the offending sheet metal cut out, the remaining portion is plug welded to the doorsill.

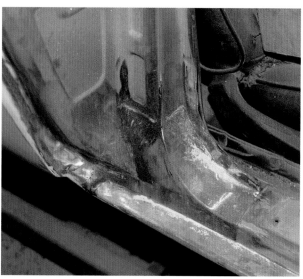

No commercially manufactured replacement panels are available for this particular area, so a handmade patch was fabricated and then welded in place.

As with most other replacement panels, you must determine how much of the old panel can be removed. Then cut out the damaged area with a plasma cutter, die grinder, air saw, tin snips, or whatever tool to which you have access. The replacement panel should then be tack welded in place to verify correct alignment. You will need to confirm that the door will actually open and close without rubbing on the rocker panel. After determining that the rocker panel is aligned properly, spot weld or stitch weld the rocker panel in place.

Floors

Consisting of two or more sheet-metal panels that are flanged to overlap, floor panels are prime targets for the formation of rust. Although seam sealer from the factory will prevent moisture and dirt from finding their way between these panels for awhile, the seam sealer will deteriorate eventually due to constant exposure to the elements. When it does, road salt from winter weather and rainwater, along with dirt and debris, will work their way between these panels and start the corrosion process.

The new floor for this vintage GTO is not finished, but it is well underway. The 18-gauge sheet metal has been cut to the basic size and shape.

Rather than form the floor in one piece with a transmission hump in the middle, floor panels are made for each side. The transmission hump will be formed out of multiple pieces, and then welded to the floor panels.

Replacement floor panels are becoming more widely available thanks to a growing automotive aftermarket. Even if replacement panels are not available for your particular vehicle, making new panels is not beyond the abilities of an amateur body worker who has some basic metalworking skills. Granted, some vehicle floors are considerably simpler than others. Since you will be beginning with flat sheet metal, you should use poster board or other similar material to make patterns, and then transfer the patterns to the sheet metal before cutting the metal. Rather than attempt to cut out one piece of sheet metal and form it to fit the entire area, consider using several pieces, each with simpler bends, and then weld them together as required.

You should also utilize some method to stiffen the floor so that it does not "oil can" or flex. This can be done by rolling a series of beads into the floor panel with a bead roller or by attaching sheet-metal hat channels to the underside. A hat channel is a piece of sheet metal that has three sides forming a channel, with a brim on the outside

The marks on the doorsill indicate where hat channels will be installed on the underside of the new floor panels. Whenever you are constructing a new floor, you need to incorporate some method of stiffening the floorboard. This can be done with hat channels welded on from the bottom or by bead rolling stiffening ribs into the floor panels.

This detail photo shows that the new floor panel is tack welded to the rocker panel. Additionally, lines indicating placement of the hat channels to the underside of the floor panel are extended from the rocker panel to the new floor panel. Holes have already been punched into the floor panel so that the hat channels can be plug welded.

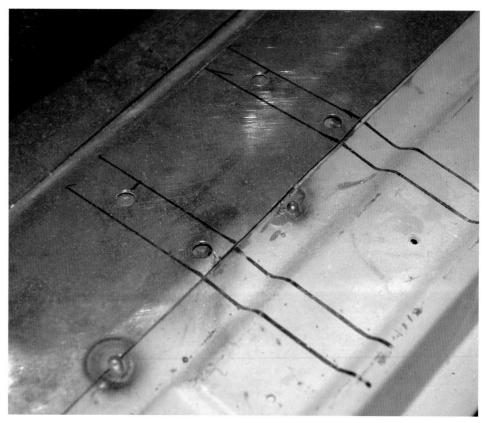

Although difficult to distinguish in this photo, this trunk floor is actually made up of three separate panels due to its size. All three are welded to the sheet metal toward the front that rises above the rear axle, as well as at the back to the tail panel.

These pieces of sheet metal are hat channels, as their profile resembles a hat. When they are plug welded across the new floor panel, the floor will be reinforced substantially.

on each side being formed by the fourth and fifth sides. This brim can then be welded or riveted to the underside of the floor.

PANEL REPLACEMENT

Panel replacement differs from patch panel installation, as you are typically installing a complete panel, such as a fender, deck lid, hood, or door skin. This may be a brand-new panel, a reproduction panel, or a used panel from a salvage yard or another parts vehicle. For the most part, panel replacement can be completed with ordinary hand tools and without welding.

Fenders

If you are fortunate enough to have a vehicle that is well supported by the aftermarket, installing a new replacement fender is pretty simple compared to hammering out a series of dents or removing rust. Front fenders for most vehicles manufactured in the last half of the twentieth century are reasonably priced, making their replacement more feasible than repair if the damage is indeed significant. Of course, minor damage can still be repaired, especially if there is no rust.

In general, fender replacement is merely a bolt-in operation, although you may need to install shims to obtain the correct alignment with other body panels. Additionally, you will most likely be required to remove some items such as the hood hinge, side marker lights, and the insignia from the old fender and reinstall them on the new fender.

REPLACING A TAIL PAN

The tail pan is the section of sheet metal across the back of the vehicle that connects both of the rear quarter panels. It is usually also connected to the trunk floor. All of these areas are susceptible to the collection of moisture and dirt, and therefore often require replacement. Keith Moritz and his crew at Morfab Customs were in the process of doing a fair amount of sheet-metal work on an early Chevrolet Camaro. The tail pan is replaced as follows . . .

Above: *The outer tail pan has been removed, leaving the inner tail pan in place. Replacement quarter panels have also been installed. The lower portion of the quarter panels is clamped to the inner tail pan.*

Right: *After double-checking and verifying proper alignment of the inner tail pan and quarter panels, the quarter panels are plug welded to the inner tail pan.*

Brent Schmelz (left) and Keith Moritz hold the outer tail pan in place and look for possible fitment issues. Even though the outer tail pan is light, its span really requires two people to check for proper alignment and fitment.

Although this is a new replacement panel, new products are not always perfect. Even if this new panel was perfect when leaving the factory, it is quite possible that some of the thin flat mounting flanges got a little out of shape and now require a little bit of hammer and dolly work to correct them.

Again, the outer tail pan is slid into place and checked for proper fit. You will find that most panels are going to require some minor modifications before fitting correctly. Still, oftentimes it is easier than repairing collision damage and much more feasible than repairing rust damage.

With the panel clamped roughly into position, the passenger side still requires a little bit of persuasion from the back end of a hammer to be positioned correctly.

Meanwhile on the driver side, some extra material is being cut off with a die grinder. Quite often, replacement panels will have some extra material. If, for instance, the quarter panels had been incorrectly installed so that they were too far apart at the back, this extra material on the tail pan would be beneficial to help tie the three pieces together. However, when the quarter panels are installed correctly, the extra tail pan material must be removed.

Above: *Still some additional material must also be removed from the tail pan. In this case, Brent is using a pneumatic reciprocating saw (a.k.a. air saw).*

Below: *Back on the passenger side, Keith is using an angle head grinder to remove the paint and primer from the outside of the inner tail pan in preparation for plug welding the outer tail pan to it.*

Keith uses an air saw to do a little bit of trimming on the passenger side as well.

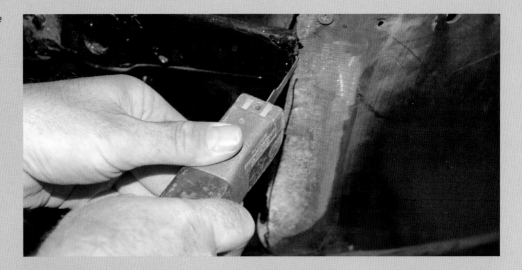

With the excess metal removed, the outer tail pan fits into the opening much better.

With the tail pan clamped into place, now is the time to verify that everything fits as it should. It is much easier to spend a little bit of time checking now before it is welded in place, rather than later when it would need to be cut out.

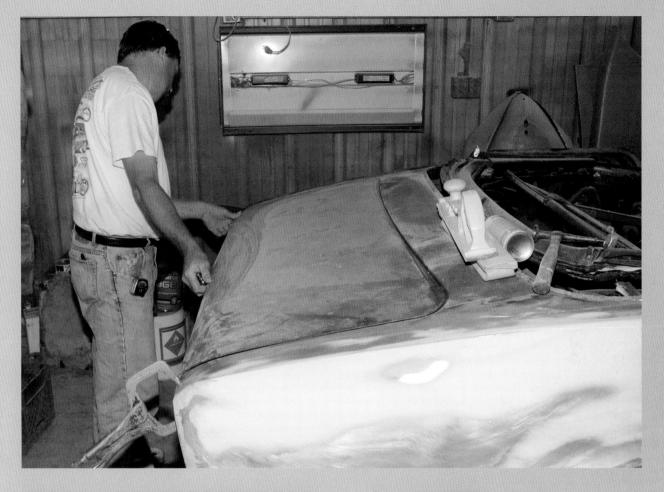

Above: *Keith checks the fit of the deck lid and the gaps between it and the newly installed quarter panels.*

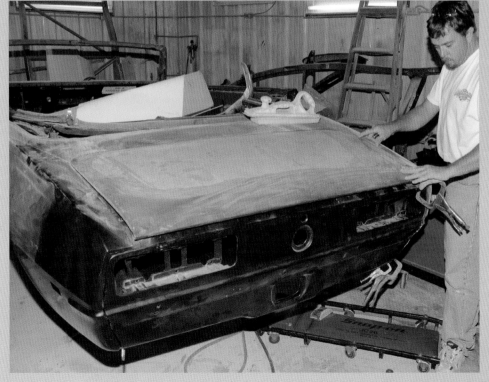

Left: *After making some minor adjustments, the gaps are checked again. Check and adjust, and check again until the fit is correct.*

149

In addition to being stitch welded around the perimeter, the outer tail pan will be plug welded to the inner tail pan in a few places. To help secure the outer tail pan into position with the inner tail pan prior to welding, a bolt is inserted into a common hole in the two and tightened with a washer and nut.

An angle head grinder is then used to remove the primer from the inner and outer tail pan around the perimeter where the two will be stitch welded together.

Below: Using a MIG welder, Keith then begins the task of welding the outer tail pan in place. Take your time and skip around from one side to the other to minimize any possible heat distortion.

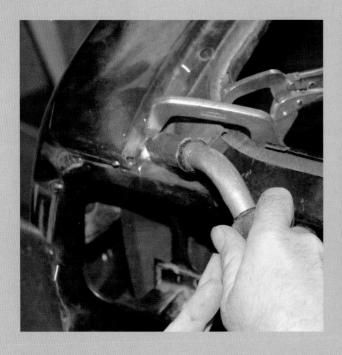

Begin the welding process by placing several tack welds around the perimeter so that the panel stays in place, just in case someone inadvertently removes the clamps.

At the top of the photo is a series of stitch welds, while a couple of tack welds can be seen lower in the photo. Eventually, stitch welds will go around the entire perimeter.

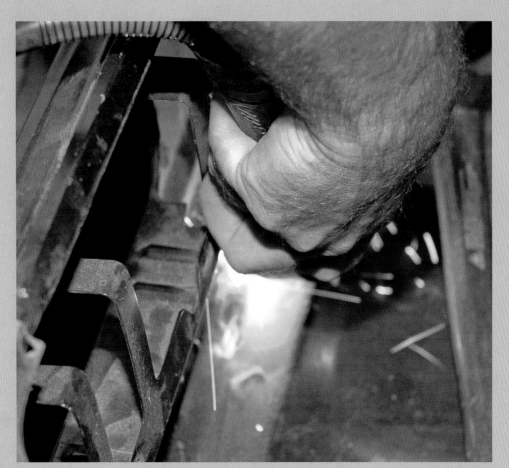

Near the middle of the inner and outer tail pans, there are some matching holes where the two are to be plug welded together. Although somewhat difficult to see in the photo, this is what Keith is doing here.

Right: *The new tail pan is essentially installed. There is still some more welding to do, but that will take awhile to complete.*

Below: *After all of the welding is completed, the various substrates prior to paint application can be applied.*

REPLACING A FENDER

Brent Schmelz at Morfab Customs was performing the preliminary fit up of a pair of replacement fenders on the front of an early Camaro convertible during a recent visit to Morfab Customs. This particular vehicle is undergoing a complete restoration, but will be using some original parts along with some replacement parts, making it typical of what you might face during a collision repair job.

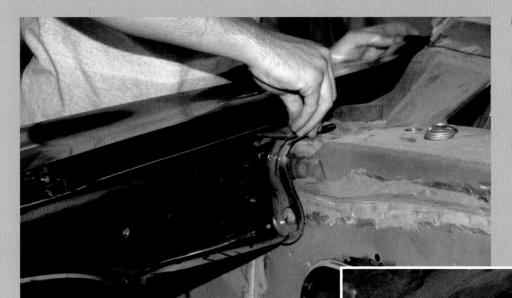

Left: *Front fenders will typically mount to the cowl and the radiator support, as well as to various other locations. The mounting locations on the cowl will usually be designed so that they can provide vertical and horizontal adjustment through the use of shims.*

Right: *The front portion of the fender is secured to the radiator support with two bolts. Some vehicles will have bolts that thread into nuts on the bottom side of the mounting location, while others will require a washer and nut to secure the mounting bolt.*

Left: *After securing the fender to the radiator support, the fender can be pushed or pulled to align the mounting holes at the cowl. You should loosely install all of the mounting bolts with a couple of turns by hand, before tightening any of them.*

The opposite side fender is installed by using the same methods.

The hood springs are then secured by installing the original hardware in the proper mounting holes in the new fender. Hood hinge mounting locations will vary from make and model, so you may need to refer to your notes made during disassembly.

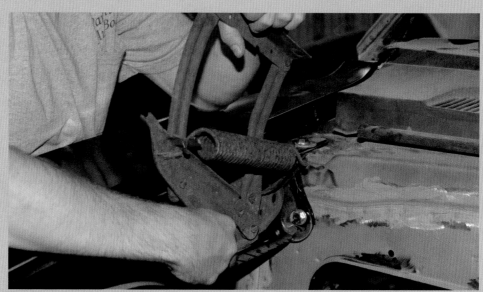

The hood is then secured to the hood hinge. Do yourself a favor and ask someone for assistance when you are installing a hood. Trying to install a hood by yourself is just making the job more difficult than it has to be.

Typically, the hood is secured to the hinge with just two or three bolts on each side. Get them all started by hand and then tighten them all.

You can then close the hood to check for proper alignment with the fenders. Be sure to let the hood down gently, and don't force it if it begins to bind. If the hinges are bound up, excessive pressure on the hood can cause it to bend. If the hinges are stiff, apply some lubricant (such as WD-40) to loosen them. If that does not work, remove the hood and hinges, clamp the hinge in a vise, apply more lubricant, tap the pivot points with a hammer, and repeat until the hinges work again.

With the hood operating freely, you should install the nose panel that spans the area between the fenders and in front of the hood.

Secure it to the fenders with bolts, washers, and nuts.

The lower fascia that spans between the fenders and under the grille should then be installed and secured to the fenders with bolts, washers, and nuts.

Above: *The fit of the fascia should be checked before tightening the mounting bolts completely.*

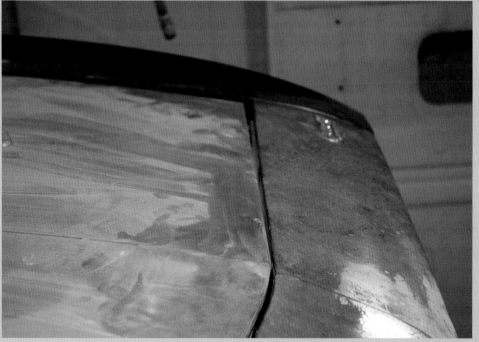

Left: *With all of the front sheet-metal components installed, the fit and alignment of the hood can be checked. As seen in this photo, the gap between the hood and the nose panel is greater near the left fender than at the center of the hood. This indicates that the left fender needs to move rearward a bit.*

Above: *Brent loosens the top bolt and then pulls the fender back toward the cowl as required. He then reinstalls and tightens the mounting bolt.*

Right: *Although all of the paint prep work still needs to be completed, it has been verified that the front clip sheet metal does fit properly. It may need some tweaking at the final assembly stage, but it is certainly within acceptable limits to proceed.*

CHAPTER 8
SURFACE PREPARATION AND UNDERCOATS

It doesn't matter if you have done bodywork to repair a severely damaged vehicle, simply hammered out a couple of small dents, or are working with brand-new, reproduction automotive sheet metal, it will require proper preparation prior to painting it. To provide the flawless paint finish that your vehicle had when it rolled off the showroom floor, you will need to apply various layers of primers.

SURFACE PREPARATION

Even if collision damage or rust repair was limited to one specific area of your vehicle, you should take the time to make sure the rest of the body is as perfect as can be prior to repainting. Your freshly repaired fender is not going to improve the looks of the collection of minor parking lot dents in the door. Now is the time to locate all of the little (or not so little) dents, dings, and scratches that may have been annoying you for a while. After all, if you have made collision repairs successfully, fixing these minor blemishes will be relatively easy.

Filling Holes

Occasionally, you will need to fill small holes in sheet metal. These usually are not the result of collision or rust, but because trim has been removed and not used again. As long as the hole is no larger than about $1/4$ inch in diameter, you can simply weld the hole shut. After it is welded closed, grind off any excess that is above the surface and then sand smooth. If the holes are larger than $1/4$ inch in diameter, cut out small pieces of sheet metal, place them over the hole from the back side, and then weld them in place. Again, grind off any excess weld and then sand smooth.

Filling Low Spots

Many minor door dings can be eliminated without using a body hammer. If the dent is less than about $1/8$ inch deep, you can eliminate it by filling it with body filler. Begin by scuffing the paint in the area to be filled down to bare metal or epoxy primer. If you have multiple dents to fill, go ahead and remove the paint from all of the divots. Scoop

The rear fender on the author's 1955 Chevy pickup project is in relatively good condition. It is not perfect, however, as it has a relatively minor dent, which can be hammered out, and a row of holes just above the bodyline. The holes are small enough that they can simply be welded shut, ground smooth, and then covered with a skim coat of body filler.

an appropriate amount of body filler onto a mixing board, but don't mix more than you can apply before it will begin to set. Apply the appropriate amount of hardener and use a plastic spreader to thoroughly mix the filler and hardener material until it has consistent color throughout and no streaks. Use the plastic spreader to apply the filler to the dent, using a wiping motion in one direction across the dent. If done properly, the filler will stay in the dent and wipe off the area around it. Use this same method to fill the rest of the dents.

After the filler begins to cure, use some 80- or 100-grit sandpaper on a sanding block to knock off any high spots of filler from around the dent. If you leave a gouge in the filler, it needs some additional time to cure. If sanding causes dust, you can continue sanding until the dent is sanded down to the correct level. If necessary, you can apply a second coat of filler to completely fill the area. After rough shaping with 80- or 100-grit sandpaper, sand the entire area with finer sandpaper until it is blended in to the surrounding area.

Sanding

You can't really sand too much, but if you don't know what you are doing, you can certainly create more problems than you will solve. Keeping in mind that you need to (1) use a sanding block or board, (2) use the appropriate grit sandpaper, and (3) sand in an "X" pattern, sanding is pretty easy. All too often, though, amateur body workers get lazy, tired, or try to cut corners, only to minimize the positive effects of their hard work.

Many amateurs waste their sanding efforts by using the palm of their hand instead of spending 10 bucks for a sanding block. For sanding to be done efficiently, the sandpaper must make full, even contact with the surface. If you squeeze your hand in several places, you will find that it is relatively soft in the palm, but harder at the knuckles and joints. Even though your hand can move the sandpaper across the body surface, more pressure will be applied at the knuckles than at the palm. This will cause waves in the panel due to the uneven pressure on the sandpaper.

The appropriate grit sandpaper for the surface being smoothed depends on whether you are smoothing body filler, color sanding paint, or somewhere in between. The table below will help you decide how rough or fine to go. (Sandpaper is also discussed in Chapter 2.)

Remain aware of where you are in the process whenever you pick up a piece of sandpaper to avoid gouging up a surface that's ready for a finer cut.

Another amateur mistake is to sand in a simple back and forth motion, causing a flat spot or gouge in the process. The correct method in which to sand is in an "X" pattern. You can do this by pushing the sander sideways as you make several diagonal passes over the surface, and then push the sander back across the area with the sander turned approximately 90 degrees from the first pass. This helps to ensure that the entire area is leveled and smoothed evenly.

Sandpaper Grit	Primary Use
36-50	Removing paint or old body filler prior to repair
80-100	Initial smoothing of plastic body filler
120-150	Block sanding polyester spray body filler
180-200	Block sanding to remove waves in sheet metal that does not have filler
200-240	Secondary smoothing and blending of body filler into surrounding (un-filled) area Also used for scuffing replacement panels (sheet metal or fiberglass) to promote adhesion
320-400	Block sanding primer-surfacer that has been applied over filled areas
400-500	Block sanding overall area to be repainted, after bodywork but prior to applying sealer
1000	Color (or wet) sanding final paint after proper curing time
1000-3000	Polishing final paint

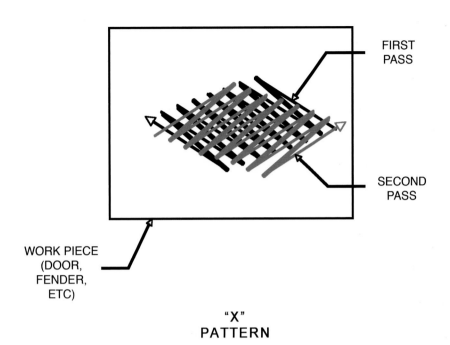

FIRST PASS

SECOND PASS

WORK PIECE
(DOOR,
FENDER,
ETC)

"X"
PATTERN

To eliminate the tendency to sand a groove in the panel you are working on, move the sanding board back and forth at approximately 45 degrees from the direction you are moving across the panel. Then, as you work back across the panel, move the sanding board back and forth at approximately 90 degrees to your original sanding pattern.

Getting It Flat and Smooth

When doing bodywork, your objective is to get the repaired panels as straight and flat as possible. This doesn't mean that you are trying to remove original bodylines. You are simply (at least in theory) trying to make the surface as smooth and blemish-free as possible. We have all seen natural lakes or manmade reflecting pools that mirror the image of the surroundings. Being liquid, water in these lakes or pools is "flat," allowing it to reflect perfectly. If you toss a rock or coin in the water and disrupt the flat surface, the reflected image is distorted, even if just temporarily. Having body surfaces that are flat will yield the most brilliant paint and allow for the brightest shine. Any imperfections that you can find now will be greatly magnified after applying a new coat of paint.

To obtain this flat surface, move sanding boards and blocks in all directions. Do not simply maneuver them in a back and forth direction from the front to the back; also move them up, down, crossways, and diagonally, rotating the board or block as necessary for ease of operation. This multidirectional sanding technique will guarantee that all areas are sanded smooth without grooves or perceivable patterns.

When satisfied that your filler repair has been sanded to perfection with 240-grit sandpaper, use 320-grit paper to gradually develop a well-defined visual perimeter around the entire repair area. This ring around the repair should expose about an inch-wide band of bare metal and then successive bands of equally wide exposed rings of primer, sealer, primer-surfacer, and paint. Because undercoat and paint products consist of different colored materials, you will be able to see your progress clearly. The object essentially is to develop sort of a layered valley of smooth walls between the top surface of the body filler area and the top surface of existing good paint. This allows fresh applications of undercoat material to fill to the same thickness as those same materials existing on the rest of the car's surface. This "feathering in" process is an important step toward successfully completing any touch-up repaint work. Subsequent coats of primer-surfacer material will also be sanded to a point where the only depth difference between an existing painted surface and a repair area will be the actual thickness of the existing paint. Sanding up to this point should have any body filler shaped to the correct contour to match the panels around it.

Masking

Masking tape will not stick to dirty, greasy, or wax covered surfaces. Although it might stick initially, it will lose its adhesion when hit with air pressure or exposed to primer or paint. So, before you begin masking, make sure you spend plenty of time washing those areas where tape will be placed.

Prior to spraying any primer-surfacer on the repaired areas, mask off anything that is not to receive primer. Although newspaper has been used in the past to mask, it should be avoided nowadays. Newsprint does not hold

By sanding in as many different directions as you can, you can eliminate waves and actually get the panel flat. Even though this pickup truck has lots of contours, the reflections in the paint indicate that the panels are flat as water of a reflecting pool.

up well against the solvents in paint and primer materials, making its use a risky proposition. Masking paper is available wherever you purchase your primer and paint products and is relatively inexpensive in light of its ease of use and effectiveness.

Masking paper and automotive grade masking tape should be used to mask the areas that are in the direct path of the application of primer or paint. To cover larger areas that are not in the direct path of primer or paint, you can use large plastic masking material that is available at retailers of automotive paint products. This material is very thin and is similar to food wrapping material. The thick plastic sheeting used as a paint drop cloth when painting the inside of your house is much too thick and heavy for use on automobiles. Although your initial estimate of the masking needs for your vehicle may appear to be rather limited and easy to accomplish, you must understand that less than meticulous masking will almost always result in obvious spots of overspray. Those imperfections will clearly indicate sloppy work or will be regarded as signs of inexperience. Some paint overspray can be cleaned off, but proactive masking is much easier than reactive cleaning.

Next to color matching, masking is perhaps the most meticulous and exacting chore required of an auto body painter. Since your auto body paint and supply store will mix paint blends and tints, your most precise work revolves around masking. To make the job as simple as possible, devise and follow a systematic masking plan, and then allot enough time to complete those tasks with strict attention to detail.

Painting panels that are located near windows always present more of a problem when masking, as there are usually several pieces of molding and trim surrounding the glass. Of course, the most efficient way to avoid errant application of paint is to remove the trim, molding, and glass, but that isn't always a practical solution—not least because you still would have to stop it from getting into the vehicle's interior. To mask these window areas, do yourself a favor and purchase a roll or two of $1/8$-inch Fine Line masking tape, in addition to the automotive grade masking tape and masking paper that will be required for the job.

Outline the area to be masked with $1/8$-inch Fine Line tape, making sure that this tape covers the very edges. Now you should attach $3/4$-inch automotive grade masking tape to the Fine Line tape. For narrow areas such as window trim, one or two additional strips of tape will probably cover the area to be masked. If you are masking a large area, secure masking paper to the first piece of $^3/_4$-inch masking tape. Be sure to use masking tape to cover any seams in masking paper.

When masking window glass, only one piece will be necessary as long as the masking paper is wide enough to reach from the top to the bottom. Fold the paper as necessary so that it fits neatly along the sides of the glass. Use strips of masking tape to hold the masking paper in place. If the glass you are masking is wider than the masking paper, use two or three strips of masking paper placed horizontally to cover all of the glass. Always run lines of tape along the length of paper edges to completely seal off underlying areas. This is especially important when the edge of one piece of masking paper is lapped over another. Lightly secured paper edges will blow open during spray paint operations and allow mists of overspray to infiltrate these underlying spaces.

Masking paper does not always come in widths that fit window shapes exactly. Most of the time, especially with side windows, you end up with a tight fit along edges and bulges in the middle. To avoid bulges, fold excess masking paper so that it lays flat. Not only does this make for a tidy masking job, it prevents bulky paper from being blown around by air pressure from a paint spray gun. All you have to do is lay one hand down on an edge of the paper and slide it toward the middle. With your other hand, grasp the bulging paper and fold it over. Use strips of tape to hold it in a neat fold.

If the windshield or back window is secured by large, flexible rubber molding, masking it can be made easier by sliding a length of soft, non-scratching cord under it. This will elevate the rubber molding up away from the surface to be painted, which will allow you to apply masking tape to the underneath edge and wrap it around the top of the molding.

Although most painting jobs call for the removal of emblems and badges, there are two occasions when they can be left in place. This is when only clear coat paint will be sprayed over them, and when spot painting work will require only a light melting coat be applied close to their edges. In either case, intricate masking with tape is needed to ensure that emblem and badge edges are completely covered and that no part of the tape extends over onto the painted surface. You have to take your time placing tape over item edges first, before masking their faces. Again, Fine Line tape may be the best choice of material for this meticulous task. After attaching the tape's end to a corner of an emblem, maneuver the roll with one hand while carefully placing and securing the tape with your other hand. Practice is essential, so do not expect to accomplish this kind of unique masking on the first try.

Some painters make this job easier by covering emblems with wide strips of tape first. A sharp razor blade is then used to cut tape along the emblem edges at the exact point where they meet the painted body. You must use a very delicate touch to avoid cutting into paint or missing the mark and leaving an open gap along the part being masked off. If you decide to try this technique, make very light passes with the razor blade, even if it takes two or three attempts to cut completely through the tape. This will prevent excessive pressure on the razor blade from cutting deeply into the sheet metal.

Since door locks and handles mount directly to door panels, the same kind of meticulous masking is required for them as for emblems and badges. If possible, door locks and handles should be removed to ensure uniform coverage of primer and paint on the door surface. If removal is not feasible, use $^3/_4$-inch tape to mask the perimeter edges and then 2-inch tape to cover the unit completely. Remember, the most critical part of masking is along the edges where items meet painted panels. Wide strips of tape can easily cover faces and other easy-to-reach parts.

Key locks are easiest to mask by simply covering them with a length of 1-inch- or 2-inch-wide tape. Use your fingernail to force tape down along the circumference to be sure coverage is complete and the tape is securely in place. Then cut the excess from around the lock's circumference with a sharp razor blade.

Do not forget to mask doorjambs before spraying primer and paint. You would be surprised how much paint can find its way between a closed door and the doorjamb. If your bodywork calls for priming and painting of door edges and doorjambs, these edges should be painted first and allowed to dry. After they have cured sufficiently for masking tape and paper to be applied, mask off the inside portion of the door and the doorjamb. You can then close the door and prime and paint the exterior.

This same procedure should be used if you are replacing the doors. It is much easier to paint the interior side and perimeter edges of doors while they are off the vehicle. You can then install the doors, mask off the door edges and doorjambs, and paint the exterior panel along with the rest of the body.

Some painters like to apply 2-inch tape along the edges of rear doorjambs with the sticky side facing out. Only about half of the tape strip actually goes on the jamb, while the rest is folded over so that it is perpendicular. Another strip is placed on the rear door edge in the same manner, with half of it protruding out with the sticky side facing out. This way, when the door is closed, both strips of tape are attached to each other to effectively seal the gap between the door and jamb.

The same technique is used along the lower door edge. For front doors, apply tape to the front edge of the rear door to match the rear edge of the front door when it is closed. A little practice and some patience are required to perfect these maneuvers. Tape does not always stick the way you would like it to, and sometimes the air movement caused by a door closing is enough to throw off the tape's ability to match up with a corresponding strip.

You can use 2-inch tape and 4- to 6-inch paper to mask doorjambs and edges; however, be careful of where you place the tape edges. If set too far out, they may allow a paint line to be visible through the gap between the door and the jamb. This is an important factor when painting a color on the exterior that is in contrast with the shade on the doorjambs. You will have to decide where the dividing line will be and make sure that tape is positioned symmetrically.

When masking drip rail molding, you must pay close attention to the top inner side, as well as the facing portion. Place tape of an adequate width to the inner side first and then lay it down over the face. Should another strip be needed, apply it to the bottom edge first and fold the excess over the front to overlap the previous strip.

Masking other types of trim does not require any special skill other than patience and attention to detail. Edges next to body panels should be covered first and the face covered last. Hold a roll of tape in one hand and position the extended strip with the other directly on top of trim sections. Be absolutely certain that trim edges are covered and that tape does not extend onto the body. Small pieces of tape that do touch body parts will block paint from the surface and cause a blemish.

Rather than wrap a radio antenna with masking tape in a "barber pole" fashion, sandwich the antenna with two strips of masking tape that are pressed together along the antenna's length. Then secure these two pieces with additional tape that also covers the antenna's base.

Taillights and side marker lights are usually easier to remove than to mask. Simply remove the necessary mounting screws, unplug the light bulb, and set the taillight assembly aside. Make sure that you mask the wires and the bulb so that you don't look like an amateur. Should you decide to mask taillights instead of removing them, plan to

use strips of 2-inch tape. Due to their designs commonly featuring curved corners or awkward shapes, masking is accomplished much easier, faster, and more completely by placing overlapping strips of 2-inch tape over their entire surface. Be sure that each overlap extends to at least $3/4$ inch to prevent paint seepage into seams. Side marker lights are masked off using the same procedure as for emblems and badges.

If you need to prime or paint the area directly behind a bumper, you should remove the latter to allow complete access, rather than masking it and spraying around it. If you are simply protecting the bumper from overspray, fold masking paper over the top edge of the bumper and tape it in place. Wrap the paper over the face of the bumper and fold the paper so that it wraps around the lower edge. Then tape the bottom edge and the seams.

To mask the front grille of your vehicle, open the hood and tape a piece of masking paper across the top of the grille so that the paper hangs down in front. Trim or fold the paper as needed, and then tape the edges of the paper along the edge of the grille. If additional pieces of masking paper are necessary, be sure to cover the seams with masking tape.

On vehicles that have painted fender wells, take time to adequately cover them with masking paper and tape. If your car has normal everyday driver fender wells covered with undercoat, you do not need to mask them unless you want to. On those, cover overspray imperfections with new layers of undercoat or black paint.

Plastic covers for wheels and tires are available to mask them from overspray, but large plastic trash bags will also work. Just be sure to secure the bags so that they do not come off during your spraying session. If you do inadvertently get some paint on your tires, scrub them clean with the same paint reducer that you are using with your paint.

Always inspect your masking work after tape has been positioned. Use a fingernail to guarantee tape is securely attached along edges. On the bottom sides of body side trim, you may have to lie down in order to place masking tape accurately. Do whatever it requires to mask your car properly, in order to accomplish your goal of having nobody being able to notice that any paintwork has been done, except that the car body looks great.

UNDERCOATS

Just because the dents have been hammered out and a coat of body filler applied does not mean that you are ready to spray paint. Oh, you could, but if you were to apply paint

This masking of a gas filler opening may not be very impressive to most. However, taking a little extra time to mask this properly will prevent you from having new paint and primer on the gas cap and the filler neck. Not a big deal, but it is something that will separate those who seek professional results from the amateurs who do not care.

At around $75, a masking paper dispenser may be beyond justification for a one-time repair, but if you do a lot of masking for priming or painting, it can save you lots of time. It applies masking tape to one edge of the paper as it is dispensed, making the paper easier to secure as you put it in place. More expensive models contain various widths of paper.

at this point, the finished vehicle would look like a spotted mess, and not have the smooth finish that your vehicle had just before the accident. If you have performed all of the necessary bodywork and done it correctly, now is certainly not the time to lose sight of finishing the task completely. Even if you cannot justify painting the affected area for whatever reason (matching body panels don't matter to you, you don't have a place to apply paint, or you simply cannot afford the paint), at least apply a uniform coat of primer to the repaired area.

Undercoats should not be confused with the thick, black, sticky tar substance that is applied to the underside of new vehicles to minimize rust-through. For the purposes of auto body repair, undercoats are the necessary substrates of various primers that precede paint and other topcoats (which are discussed in detail in Chapter 9). Undercoats provide basic corrosion protection to bare metals, increase adhesion of the substrates or topcoats to follow, and provide a surface that can be sanded smooth. Since undercoats in general perform a multitude of tasks, specific types of primers must be used for each step of the priming process.

Cleaning

After sanding or scuffing the surface, a thorough cleaning is required to remove all contaminants. Painters normally use air pressure to blow off layers of sanding dust from body surfaces, as well as between trunk edge gaps, door edges, and doorjambs.

With the bulk of dry dust and dirt removed by air pressure, painters use wax and grease remover products to wipe down and clean body surfaces thoroughly. Each paint manufacturer has its own brand of wax and grease remover that constitutes part of an overall paint system. You should use only those wax and grease remover products deemed part of your chosen paint system to guarantee that it is compatible with the rest of the materials.

Dampen a clean cloth (heavy-duty paper shop towels work great) with wax and grease remover and use it to wipe off thoroughly all body surfaces in the area of expected paint undercoat applications. The mild solvents in wax and grease removers loosen and dislodge particles

MASKING

Whether you are going to repair and repaint your damaged vehicle or just make it drivable and spray on some primer, you will need to mask off the areas where you don't want primer and paint. You may simply be masking off the glass before repainting the entire body, or limiting the new paintwork to just a localized area, such as two doors and a fender. Follow along as one of the body men from Jerry's Auto Body masks a four-door sedan prior to applying primer-surfacer.

Prior to masking the outside of the vehicle, wipe it down with wax and grease remover. Just as paint will not stick to dirt and other contaminants, neither will masking tape. You for sure do not want the masking tape and paper to start coming loose when you are in the middle of spraying primer-surfacer, or even worse while spraying the final paint.

Prior to masking, you must take a moment to determine what actually needs to be masked and what needs to be left open. From about the middle of the front door to the edge of the body where it meets the rear bumper/fascia, and from the bottoms of the windows to the bottom edge must be left open. So, first use a piece of wide masking paper to cover the front half of the front door. For primer-surfacer application, this wide piece of masking paper will provide sufficient coverage for the front portion of the car. Additional masking will be necessary when the topcoat of paint is applied.

Attach a piece of tape to the bottom edge of the car from the inside, so that you can attach a piece of masking paper to it later. This will act as a skirt to prevent overspray from hitting the underside of the vehicle.

Now open the front door and place tape along the inner edge of the door. Tape the masking paper to this first piece of tape and then fold it to the inside of the door. This will protect the doorjamb and doorpost from overspray through the gap between the doors.

Repeat this same procedure of masking the doorjamb on the back door as well. Taking the time to do this carefully will ultimately save you more time in the long run, as you will not need to come back and sand off overspray from the doorjambs.

Although it is a relatively small opening, it is still necessary to close up the hole caused by removing the outside door handle, as a lot of primer-surfacer can find its way inside the car. This opening is not being masked off from paint application, as all of the outside should be coated with primer-surfacer, and then paint. For this reason, you have to mask it from the inside, instead of the outside as with the windows. With the door open, and the interior door panel removed, you can overlap two pieces of wide masking tape to close off this opening.

Even though there may seem to be no reason for removing the interior door panels, tasks like closing the opening due to the removal of the door handle make it a necessity. Some people may just leave the interior door panel in place and use it to prevent paint from getting inside the car. That, however, would be a very unprofessional way of doing the work.

With the interior door panel removed, you can get a glimpse of the inside of the door. Shown are the window riser mechanism (do not pinch your fingers), the connecting rod to the door latch, and wiring for power door locks.

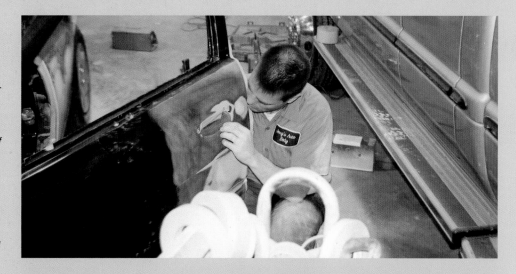

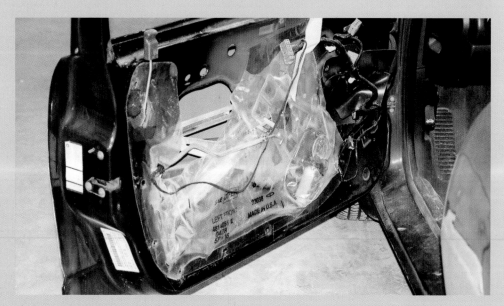

With a skirt along the bottom of the vehicle, you can now mask off the windows with masking paper. Do not apply primer-surfacer above the bottom edge of the windows or above that imaginary line, as it would cross the rear quarter panel. Therefore, align the masking paper with the lower edge of the window only and simply drape it over the window, instead of specifically masking the glass area.

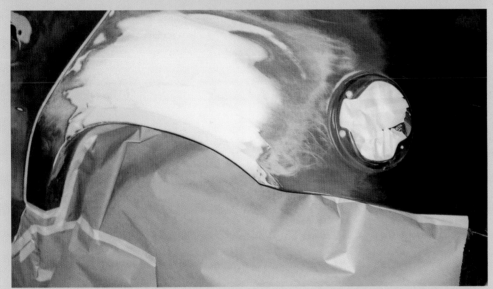

Much like the opening in the door for the door handle, the gas filler door must be masked from behind as well. Apply the masking tape to the inner edge of the wheelwell to serve as an attachment point for masking paper to cover the wheel and tire. Fold the paper over as necessary to completely cover the wheel and tire, yet still be out of the way so that the wheelwell is accessible to be painted.

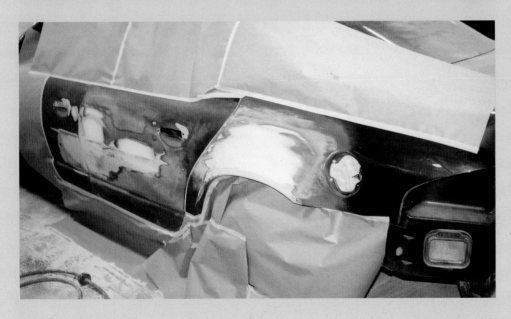

This Dodge sedan is almost masked sufficiently for the application of primer-surfacer. It should be noted that primer-surfacer will extend beyond the actual repair area, yet not completely to the masked edge. When doing the actual painting, paint the entire left rear quarter panel, along with both doors. To fully match the rest of the car, it may be necessary to blend clear onto the trunk, the roof, and the front fender.

For a guide coat, almost any contrasting color of spray-can enamel can be used. It should be sprayed on lightly and uniformly.

If the guide coat is indeed sprayed on uniformly, the panel should be flat (without ripples) when all of the guide coat is sanded off.

of silicone dressings, oil, wax, polish, and other materials embedded in, or lightly adhered to, surfaces. To assist the cleaning ability of wax and grease removers, follow the damp cleaning cloth with a clean, dry cloth in your other hand. The dry one picks up lingering residue and moisture to leave behind a clean, dry surface. Use a new towel on every panel, wipe wet, and dry *thoroughly*.

Primer-Surfacer

An application of primer-surfacer will quickly provide you with visual evidence of how complete you have done your bodywork. What may look great when still in bare metal or body filler will now show every low spot, high spot, or other blemish. Although primer-surfacer is often referred to as high build primer, it should not be used as body filler.

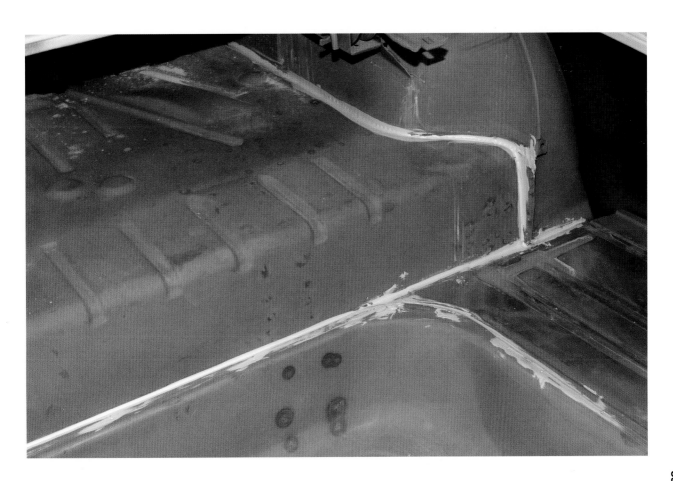

Seam sealer, which looks much like caulking found around your bathtub or sink, has been applied to the seams of this early 1960s Chevrolet trunk. Since this large area comprises several smaller pieces of sheet metal that are welded together, there is more than ample opportunity for moisture, dirt, and debris to find their way between the overlap of these panels. The seam sealer keeps this from happening and therefore minimizes the opportunity for rust to form.

If there are indeed low spots that need to be filled, you should use additional body filler.

Begin by cleaning the area with wax and grease remover, and then use a tack rag to remove dust particles and lint. Be sure to mix the primer-surfacer and reducer per the mixing instructions on the label, and then apply two or three coats of primer-surfacer to all areas where you have done bodywork. Obviously you are wearing appropriate protective gear here and every other time you have sprayed paint products or other chemicals. Make sure that you allow the proper flash time between coats. If you have several localized spots of repair on one or adjacent panels, go ahead and apply primer-surfacer to the entire panel rather than just the spots where you have done repair work. This will allow you to better blend the surfaces during the block sanding process.

After the primer-surfacer has had ample time to cure, spray a light but uniform mist coat of SEM Guide Coat (or any contrasting color spray-can enamel) onto the areas to be sanded. After this guide coat dries, break out your favorite sanding board with some 320-grit sandpaper and block sand the entire area where primer-surfacer has been applied. The guide coat will quickly disappear from high spots, but not from low spots.

After this initial sanding with 320-grit, it should be obvious if any additional filler is required. If it is, add it as needed, shaping it with 100- and 240-grit sandpaper. Then apply two or three coats of primer-surfacer to all areas where additional filler was applied. Block sand these areas again with 320-grit sandpaper. If the body is at the proper contour after sanding with 320-grit sandpaper, switch to 500-grit sandpaper and block sand the entire area again.

Finer sandpaper grits will improve texture smoothness and remove sanding scratches as well as very shallow imperfections. Using the longest sanding board or block available with progressively finer sandpaper is the key to achieving the straightest and flattest surface upon which to apply paint.

SPRAYING PRIMER-SURFACER

Spraying primer-surfacer is easy to do, but you must do it correctly, as the rest of the paint process is based upon this step. At this point, you still have plenty of sanding to do, so you don't have to be concerned with runs and sags, as they can be sanded out during the block sanding process. For some, this will be the first time you have ever used a spray gun. You will need to adjust the gun to the recommended air pressure setting for the material you are spraying. Do some practice spraying on something before turning to your vehicle's body parts. Follow along as a sedan is prepped for paint at Jerry's Auto Body.

SURFACE PREPARATION AND UNDERCOATS

After all of the masking is completed, but before any primer-surfacer is applied, clean the area to be primed again with wax and grease remover. Although you can apply the remover with a clean paper towel and wipe it off with another, most professionals apply it with a spray bottle and then wipe off the wax and grease with a clean paper towel.

Even primer-surfacer should be carefully mixed to ensure proper application. Using a calibrated mixing cup makes mixing primer-surfacer with reducer quite easy. Be sure to read the mixing instructions to verify the correct ratio. After thorough mixing by stirring, place a paint strainer in the spray paint cup and pour in the primer-surfacer. Never pour any kind of a paint product into a spray paint cup without a strainer. Strainers are usually free from where you purchase your paint, while not using one may cost you a spray gun if a speck of dirt or debris gets into an orifice that can not be cleaned.

Sealer

Sealer is typically the last of the undercoats to be applied before color. At this point all bodywork should be completed, all sanding done, and any areas that are not to receive sealer masked off. The purpose of the sealer is as the name suggests: to seal in all of the various undercoats and fillers to keep them from seeping into the topcoats. The sealer will also provide a uniform base to allow for uniform color coverage and aid in adhesion of the topcoats.

Before applying sealer, use an air hose to blow dust and dirt out of all cracks and crevices. Clean the surface with wax and grease remover, and mask off all areas that should not receive sealer. Use the air hose on the surface again, clean again with wax and grease remover, and go over the area with a tack cloth. Mix the sealer by following the directions, set the air pressure as directed, and put on your protective gear, if not on already. Spray sealer first over the areas where filler has been applied, then feather the sealer toward the masked edges, but do not spray all the way to the edge. Allow the sealer to flash dry per the directions, and then apply second and third coats with the appropriate time between coats.

Sealer should not be sanded, unless runs or other imperfections occur. If that happens, allow the sealer to dry, use fine-grit sandpaper to remove the blemish, and touch up with more sealer. Once the sealer has cured according to label directions, paint can then be applied.

Seam Sealer

One of the reasons why vehicles rust is that many adjacent panels are simply plug welded together at the factory, and seam sealer is then applied between the welds to seal these seams. As the seam sealer eventually falls out, the plug weld allows moisture and dirt to find their way between these panels. Over time, this will cause rust and corrosion at the mating surfaces and eventually the panels will begin to fall apart. Seam sealer from the 1960s and 1970s simply was not of the same high quality as today's sealer.

When making repairs, there are two methods for preventing rust from recurring in these rust prone areas. The best way would be to minimize the opportunity by stitch welding all of the panels together. This would greatly minimize the potential of rust, as there would be no open seams to attract and accumulate dirt, debris, and moisture. If you are not actually replacing any panels or complete welding is not feasible, you can apply new seam sealer.

If the components to be sealed are going to be stripped (mechanically or chemically), this step should be done first, and then epoxy primer applied. Any existing seam sealer should be removed prior to installing new seam sealer. To apply seam sealer, the metal surfaces should be clean, but it is not necessary for any primer or paint to be removed. Seam sealer is available in a tube dispensed with a caulking gun or in a tube that can be squeezed by hand. In either case, simply apply a bead along the seam between two adjacent panels.

CHAPTER 9
PAINTING, COLOR, AND OTHER TOPCOATS

Painting an automobile—the actual practice of applying paint to the vehicle's surface—is relatively easy. Although it shouldn't be taken lightly, the process of mixing some paint pigment, reducer, and hardener together, pouring the concoction into a spray gun cup, and pulling the trigger is fairly simple. Those things will be discussed in more detail a little bit later. Regardless of what anyone else may tell you, the body straightening, block sanding, and other surface preparation is generally what makes or breaks a paint job. Sure, you could do something really stupid when applying the paint, but short of having brain fade while doing it, painting is really the easiest part of the bodywork process.

All body surface preparation jobs are related by a single goal: a perfect paint job. However, each has a direct impact on the overall outcome and has its own function, which will not improve on another's lack of perfection. So, take your time during each preparatory phase and do not go on to the next step until satisfied that the work you just did has been accomplished accurately and completely.

Auto body surface preparations include those jobs that actually get surfaces ready for paint application. Depending on the specific project, those tasks may consist of, but are not limited to: part dismantling, old paint and rust removal, application of primer material, finish sanding, and surface cleaning with wax and grease remover and tack cloths. When any of these efforts are done haphazardly, the next operation cannot possibly be accomplished correctly. These processes have all been discussed previously, so if you are feeling hesitant about your bodywork or paint prep, now may be the time to go back and reread some of these sections. Then go back and redo anything that you didn't get quite right. This may seem like lots of extra work, but it is easier to do now before you paint, rather than wait until after the paint is applied and wishing you had taken a little extra time in the preparation.

PAINT SCHEME

If you have simply repaired some minor collision damage on your daily driver, you will most likely paint the affected panels the color they were before the collision. Whether that is one color or a couple depends on your particular vehicle and to what panels the damage occurred. If you are lucky, the damage is limited to just one panel and in an area that is just one color. In reality however, Murphy's Law dictates that damage probably extends across multiple panels and involves every color imaginable. On most production vehicles that have a two-tone paint scheme, the color is usually broken at a bodyline so that masking is more easily accomplished. Additionally, there is usually some sort of trim that covers the edge of the different colors. Determine the extent of the necessary repainting efforts before you prepare to start spraying paint. All too often it is difficult for the amateur body worker to conceive just how large an area will be affected when making a repair to what first appears to be a small dent.

Not that you have to do anything different, but you must realize that anything other than a monotone paint job will require additional work. Except for detailed custom airbrush work such as on hot rods or race cars, each color of paint that is sprayed will require that the entire vehicle be masked off, except of course the area being sprayed at the time. If you have masked the vehicle properly one time, you can do it again; however, this may be more than what you care to try if this is your first time painting a vehicle.

When applying multicolors, it is even more critical to observe the proper flash and drying times for the paint system you are using prior to masking. Applying masking tape or masking paper to freshly painted surfaces that have not yet dried adequately can make a complete mess of your freshly applied paint. Product information sheets for the specific type of paint you are using will provide a specified time to allow the paint to dry before taping. Likewise, clear coats (if applicable) must be applied within a specified time, or the basecoat will need to be scuffed and additional basecoats added.

Monotone

Since the collision damage has been repaired to like-new condition, matching the paint is your biggest remaining

Although there are numerous opportunities to practice perfect masking, such as around the lights, a monotone vehicle is easier to mask for painting.

hurdle. Assuming that you are not doing a complete color change (more about that in a moment), you will need the color code for your vehicle in order to purchase the correct paint color. That information is usually included on the VIN tag or the color and options tag, which can usually be found on the driver's doorjamb, in the glove box door, or somewhere under the hood. If you can't find the tag for your vehicle, check with the folks at the shop where you plan to purchase your automotive paint. They will usually have resources that show where the color code tags are, as long as you can tell them what make and model you have.

When you take your paint code number to your paint supplier, it can put the number into its paint mixing program and provide the amount of paint you want in the color that matches what is on the rest of your vehicle. However, on occasion, the paint code does not match what is actually on the vehicle. Although the percentage of mismatched paint codes is small, with the large number of production vehicles built each year, it is still a somewhat alarming number of vehicles. It is also possible that your vehicle may have been completely repainted some-

where along the line. So, after the paint store attendant determines your factory color, but before he or she mixes a couple of gallons for you, verify that the paint is basically blue, yellow, red, or whatever you are anticipating it being. If your vehicle is blue, but the paint code turns out to be yellow, something is amiss.

For a simple monotone paint job, you can clean the vehicle with wax and grease remover, mask off what isn't going to be painted, remove any dust with a tack cloth, and then apply paint. If you are planning to do a complete color change, even a monotone paint scheme will be a bit more complicated. The majority of the additional work will be under the hood and the interior of the vehicle. The only correct way to paint under the hood requires removing the engine, as you simply don't have enough room to maneuver to mask and paint the firewall properly. On older, larger vehicles, you may be able to paint the inner fenders by using a detail spray gun. On the inside of the vehicle, you should remove everything that you possibly can so that you aren't required to mask it. Of course, many vehicles have neutral color painted surfaces that could be used as is, even if the exterior color is changed. Whether

Although this mid-1950s Chevrolet relies heavily on trim to break the multicolor layout, it still presents a challenge when masking if all of the trim has been removed. Before doing a multicolor paint job, you should make plenty of notes to make sure that you get it right on both sides.

the interior color and your new exterior color complement each other or clash is for you to decide.

Multicolor

It would seem natural to include both colors when repainting a vehicle that originally had a two-tone paint scheme. However, you should study your vehicle very closely prior to removing or priming over any of the existing paint. Where does the primary color stop and the secondary color start? Is there a piece of trim that covers this seam and will that trim piece still be used after the paint job? Does the trim cover the entire paint seam, or is some of it left out in the open? Which color are the doorjambs? How well you duplicate the original color transitions will have a great impact on your overall paint job. It is better to have a high quality monochrome paint job than a mediocre two-tone result.

Think about how you would mask the area that is to be a different color and remember that it should be the same on both sides of the vehicle. This will help you realize that you need to take advantage of bodylines and natural breaks if you are designing a two-tone paint scheme. If you are going to be hiding a paint seam under a piece of trim, be sure to split the width of the trim evenly with each color. If the trim is 1 inch wide, this leaves $^1/_2$ inch for each color. You should be able to align the trim accurately enough to cover this, but if the trim is narrower, you will have less room for error in masking or trim installation.

It does not really matter which color of a two-tone paint scheme you paint first, but you should plan ahead to make your masking work easier. When all of the bodywork is done, sealer is applied, and all areas that are not to receive any paint are masked off, no additional masking would be necessary for the first color to be applied. After applying this first color, you will need to mask it off before applying the second color. For this reason, it makes sense to spray the color to the area that is going to be easiest to mask first, whether it is the lighter or darker color.

For example, you are repainting a large four door sedan that is going to be maroon with a dark gray secondary color below a bodyline, which runs approximately through the middle of the doors. It would be easy enough to paint the lower area, mask it off, and then paint the rest of the car, rather than paint the top and attempt to mask off the larger area.

TYPES OF PAINT

Although paint application basics remain at least somewhat constant, the types of paint available have greatly changed over the years. The cheap and easy-to-use acrylic lacquer paint from a few decades ago is now a thing of the past. Likewise, plain old "one coat" acrylic enamel is gone as well. Even though those products were easy to use, their replacements are far superior in finish quality, durability, and user friendliness.

Single-Stage

Urethane enamel paint products (aka single stage) consist of a color pigment (paint) to which a prescribed amount of hardener is mixed just prior to application. By applying two or three coats of urethane enamel, a properly prepared surface will yield a high gloss finish without buffing and will provide a very durable surface. A downside is that there are less layers of material between your vehicle's body and the sometimes harsh elements of the world. In other words, if the paint layer does get scratched, it could easily expose the primer or even the bare metal, making it susceptible to rust.

Some painters believe that a single-stage paint system that is wet sanded and buffed provides a better color. This may very well be true, as many people feel that the clear of a basecoat/clear-coat system takes away some of the appearance of depth that was common in the old lacquer paint jobs. A downside of a single-stage paint system is that the layer of paint on the vehicle is going to get thinner each and every time you rub a car washing sponge, chamois, or wax applicator across it.

Basecoat/Clear-coat

If you are painting anything other than a one-color paint job, you will make your job easier by using a basecoat/clear-coat paint system. Using a basecoat/clear-coat system will allow you to apply two coats of clear over the first color in a multicolor paint scheme. If you inadvertently miss any of the first color when you are masking, slight overspray from the second color can be sanded out of the clear that is protecting the first color. After the second color (and third,

if applicable) is applied, the entire vehicle should be coated with two or three additional coats of clear.

Whether spraying one color or several, using a basecoat/clear-coat system involves more spraying time as you must apply the basecoat in enough coats to obtain coverage, and then apply the desired number of clear coats. You must allow the proper flash time between coats and then wait the proper amount of time for the basecoat to dry before applying clear. Product information sheets for your specific paint products provide all of the flash time, dry time, and application pressure information that you need. You just need to make sure that you ask for them when you purchase your paint products.

After you apply clear and it has had adequate time to dry, it can be wet sanded to remove any surface imperfections. Removing these imperfections will make the surface more optically flat, which is what provides the basis for the ultimate shine.

Tri-Stage

Originally reserved for custom paint jobs or high-end vehicles, tri-stage paint systems are becoming common on OEM paint finishes. By combining a basecoat, a color coat, and a clear coat, some exotic colors can be created, including pearls and candies.

Basecoats are usually a metallic color, such as gold or silver, but can also be black or white. The color coat can be virtually any color, but will vary in appearance depending on the base color to which it is applied. For example, a red color coat sprayed over a silver base will yield a different tint than if applied to a gold basecoat. The clear coat finish will prevent wet sanding or polishing from distorting the blended color achieved between the basecoat and color coat.

As you are applying multiple coats of three different products, the amount of time required when using a tri-stage paint system increases considerably. It is not recommended for the beginner, yet if you are doing repair work to a vehicle that has a tri-stage paint surface, it is the only way.

APPLYING PAINT

Once you have decided what color everything is to be painted, you have your paint, and the masking is done, you are finally able to start applying paint. Well, almost. Have you actually sprayed any color previously? There is a slight difference in spraying paint than primer, if for no other reason than the paint is a different consistency and requires different air pressure than primer. Using the same speed of movement and distance from the surface will

Rather than installing freshly painted parts with the ever-present risk of damaging them during the process, many painters will apply paint to only the door jambs and other edges that would be difficult to paint after installation. Then, the vehicle is reassembled and everything that is left to be painted is painted in its installed position.

work fine for one, but will have you wiping off runs and sags for the other.

Do-it-yourselfers must rely upon personal practice and trial-and-error experience. If you haven't sprayed actual paint or if it has been awhile, get an old hood, trunk lid, or door and practice before you jump in on your newly repaired bodywork. Mix paint products according to label instructions and apply them at the recommended air pressure.

Try painting with different fan patterns and pressure settings to see which combinations work best for intricate work in confined spaces and which perform better on large panels. Practice holding the spray gun perpendicular to the work surface and see what happens when you don't. Use cans of inexpensive paint, and practice until you become familiar with the techniques required for good paint coverage.

Before You Start Spraying

In the paint booth or garage, wipe off body surfaces with a tack cloth as a final cleaning chore just before spray-

ing any paint product. These specially made cloths are designed to pick up and retain very small specks of lint, dust, and other particles. Although wax and grease removers work well to get rid of contaminants, tack cloths work best for removing tiny pieces of cloth fiber and other items that could easily cause imperfections in paint finishes. Take the tack cloth out of the package, open it fully, and let it air out before using. Go over every square inch of body surface that will be exposed to paint to be certain that traces of lint are removed. This should guarantee that debris is not blown over onto painted surfaces during the paint process.

Tack cloths have a limited life span. Therefore, you need to refer to instructions on package labels to determine how many times they can be used effectively. Do not try to get more out of them than expected. Once tack cloths are saturated with lint, debris, and residue, they will no longer pick up new debris. In fact, they may spread accumulated materials absorbed from other cleaning jobs.

Applying Color

There are two basic philosophies when applying paint, and both have their advantages and disadvantages. Much of the decision is based on how much of the vehicle is going to be repainted, how much has been disassembled for repair/replacement, and how soon the vehicle needs to be drivable. Neither method is right or wrong, so it doesn't really matter which you choose.

Many builders of body-off restorations or show-oriented vehicles assemble all of the sheet metal completely to verify proper fit. The sheet metal is then disassembled as completely as possible, prepped, painted, and then reassembled for the last time. This allows for thorough accessibility during the prep and painting stages requiring minimal masking, but calls for extreme care during reassembly. Any nicks or scratches to the paint during assembly will require touchup. Also, since various components may be painted at different times, some subtle differences may appear from one component to another.

Other builders choose to prep and paint the undersides and edges of hoods, doors, and deck lids, along with the edges of fenders. The vehicle is then completely assembled, taking care to not damage any of the painted surfaces. After assembly, the already painted surfaces are masked off and the entire vehicle painted at one time. This method calls for more masking, yet requires only minimal touchup (if any) and provides uniform color on adjacent panels.

Applying Clear

The application of clear is no different from any other paint, except that it dries to a nearly invisible finish. Therefore, you must maintain a closer eye on your work so that each pass is uniform.

Instructions for mixing solvents and hardeners in with clear paint material are provided on product labels, application guides, and information sheets. Of utmost importance is respecting the proper amount of the flash time between the last color coat and application of clear. Spraying clear coats on before the solvents in color coats have sufficiently evaporated will cause checking and crazing.

AFTER APPLYING PAINT

Now that the paint has been applied, you are certainly much closer to being finished than when you first started, but there is still more work to do. If nothing else, you need to clean all of your paint spraying equipment and remove masking material from the vehicle. For a higher quality finish (if that is your intent), you will also need to wet sand any slight imperfections and buff the paint.

Cleaning Your Spray Equipment

For paint spraying equipment to function properly, it must be kept clean as the air and material passages are very small to begin with. You will need to check your local ordinances for disposal of paint materials. The general procedure for cleaning spray equipment is to pour any unused material into a container that is suitable for disposal according to your local restrictions. Then fill the paint cup about halfway full of the appropriate reducer for the material that you last sprayed. Spray this reducer at about 40 psi, occasionally shaking the paint gun gently to aid in removing partially dry material from the paint cup. Continue this procedure until only reducer is coming from the spray gun. Then use a disposable towel dipped in reducer to wipe out the paint cup, so that it has no traces of primer, paint, or clear in it. Remove the fluid tip from the front of the spray gun, and wipe the area clean with a disposable towel dipped in reducer. Now re-install the fluid tip, fill the cup about a third full of reducer again, and spray it all out until the spray gun is empty. Continue to blow air through the spray gun for a minute or two to help remove any reducer from the fluid passages.

Removing Masking Material

As anxious as you will be to see what your vehicle looks like with its new paint, you must show some restraint as you remove the masking material. If you simply tear off the masking paper and tape with reckless abandon, you will no doubt do at least some damage to the new paint. It is quite likely that some amount of paint (color or clear) will be overlapping the edge of the masking tape. If the masking tape is simply pulled straight up from the painted surface, the paint will tend to flake along the edge. To prevent this from happening, pull the tape away from the freshly painted surface and back upon itself so that the tape is leaving the surface at a sharp angle.

If several coats of color and clear have been applied to the body surface, it may be necessary to cut through the layers of paint at the edge of the tape. If you are required to do this, make sure that you use a sharp razor blade, take your time, and be careful. You don't want to damage the paint or slice open an appendage.

Wet Sanding

After the paint has had sufficient time to cure, wet sanding (sometimes referred to as "color sanding") is done to remove any texture in the paint, yielding a mirror-like finish. You should always check with the paint supplier to verify that the paint you intend to use is compatible with wet sanding.

While you may choose not to wet sand at the primer stage, the process is the same on the finish coat: wet the sandpaper and sand in a circular or orbital motion until the paint or clear (ask your paint supplier) becomes very smooth.

While urethane enamel can be wet sanded and buffed, just like clear, many of the older enamel products should not be wet sanded. As a basic rule of thumb, most paint products that are catalyzed (when hardener is added while the paint is being mixed with reducer just prior to application) can be wet sanded and buffed. As some products can be buffed after just 24 hours while others require 90 days, you should verify the necessary requirements for your paint system.

Basecoat/clear-coat or tri-stage paint systems are the typical candidates for wet sanding, as it can be performed on the clear, rather than the actual color coats. No sanding should be done to color coats in these systems, unless it is to remove runs, drips, or other errors. However, sand-ing out these defects may necessitate repainting an entire panel. Especially with candy finishes, sanding directly on the color surface will distort the tint, which will cause a visible blemish. You should concentrate your wet sanding efforts on clear coats in order to leave the underlying color coats undisturbed. Wet sanding clear coats will bring out a much deeper shine and gloss when followed by controlled buffing and polishing.

Painters use very fine 1000- to 3000-grit sandpaper with water to smooth or remove minor blemishes on cured paint finishes designed to allow wet sanding. As with all other sanding tasks, you should use a sanding block. Since nibs of dirt or dust are small, fold sandpa-

A buffer can really bring out the shine. Be careful around contours in the bodywork, however, to avoid burning through the paint.

per around a wooden paint stir stick instead of using a large hand block. The size is great for smoothing small spots, because the width of ordinary wood stir sticks is about 1 inch, which is just what is needed for the area being covered. Only a small amount of pressure is required for this type of delicate sanding. Be sure to dip sandpaper in a bucket of water frequently to keep the paint surface wet and reduce the amount of material buildup on the sandpaper. You should add a small amount of mild car washing soap to the water bucket to provide lubrication to the sandpaper. Also allow the sandpaper to soak in water for 15 minutes before wet sanding. Before sanding, you could let the

water sit in a bucket overnight, so that any minerals in the water that could cause scratches will most likely settle to the bottom.

In some cases such as on show cars, the entire car body may be wet sanded to bring out the richest, deepest, and most lustrous shine possible. Because they anticipate extensive wet sanding and polishing operations, painters of these cars make sure that they have applied plenty of clear coats. If they didn't, wet sanding would remove all of the thin clear coat material, eventually reach the color coats, and destroy an otherwise fine paint job.

To remove evidence of wet sanding, finishes are rubbed out or buffed with fine compound. This work brings out more shine and luster, as well as flattening slight hints of orange peel. For spot painting or single-panel jobs, polishing adjacent body sections may be desperately needed to bring their lightly oxidized surfaces back to the point where they shine as brilliantly as the new paint.

As meticulous as you were while masking, there may be a few body parts that exhibit signs of overspray. Before putting all of the dismantled exterior body parts back on, you may want to consider removing obvious overspray and repainting those affected areas with a proper color. In some cases, such as on fender wells, you can get away with just new coats of black paint or undercoating material. A task of this nature will be easier to accomplish while masking is still in place on the vehicle.

Buffing

Like wet sanding, you should first verify with your paint supplier that the paint system you are using is compatible with buffing, as well as its specific buffing instructions. In the case of single-stage urethane, buffing new paint with a gritty compound will actually dull the surface and ruin the finish. On the other hand, basecoat/clear-coat or tri-stage systems greatly benefit from buffing, resulting in a more brilliant finish with a much deeper shine.

Some buffing compounds are designed for use by hand, while others are designed to be used with a buffing machine. There are also different types of buffing pads, mainly foam or cloth. Some compounds should be used with a foam pad and a higher speed, while others call for a wool pad and a slower speed.

Rubbing compounds are made of relatively coarse polishing material and are designed to remove minor blemishes quickly and flatten the paint finish. (In this instance, "flatten" means to make the painted finish as perfect as possible so that it is more reflective.) Since this rubbing compound is coarse, it will leave light scratches or swirls on the painted surface. A much finer buffing compound should then be used to eliminate these fine swirls.

As refinish products have changed over the years, so have some of the ideas on buffing. With the new urethane paint products, many painters are doing their first polishing round with 2000-grit compound using a foam pad. This usually minimizes swirls and provides a satisfactory finish the first time around. If swirls are still present, they go back to a slightly coarser compound to remove the swirls, then use the finer 2000-grit again. Older technology and what we all learned in junior high wood shop regarding sandpaper would have said to use the coarse rubbing compound first, and then work up to the finer stuff, instead of this seemingly backward procedure.

To use a buffer, first spread out a few strips of compound, each about 4 to 6 inches apart, to cover an area no bigger than 2 square feet. Operate the buffing pad on top of a compound strip and work it over that strip's area, gradually moving down to pick up successive strips. The idea is to not allow the pad to become dry of compound while buffing a 2-square-foot area. Continue buffing on that section until the compound is gone and the paint is shiny, and then move onto another area. You must keep the buffer moving to keep from burning into, or even through, the paint—be especially careful near ridges and corners.

If you are using buffing compound that can be applied by hand, use a back and forth motion. This will help prevent swirls and, when you are buffing by hand, you should do whatever you can to minimize your work.

You must also remove dried compound from the buffing pad by using a pad spur. Do this by gently, but securely, pushing a spur into the pad's nap while the pad is spinning. This breaks the dried compound loose and forces it out of the pad. Just be sure to do your pad cleaning away from your car and anything else that you don't want covered with compound or pad lint.

CHAPTER 10
REASSEMBLY

By now you should be seeing some light at the end of the tunnel that is collision repair or the restoration of beautiful panels once ravaged by rust. All of the once damaged parts should be rebuilt, repaired, or replaced and refinished in the appropriate color. Any blemishes have been wet sanded, polished, and touched up. The masking material is removed and you just need to reassemble everything. Much of this will be reinstalling the various pieces and parts that are not sheet metal, such as lights and trim.

Installing various parts on car bodies must be done systematically—similar to the way they were dismantled. Certain trim sections are designed to be put on first, with part of their edge covered by the next section. Failure to follow an intended sequence the first time will require you to take off those out-of-order sections and put them back on correctly. This not only creates extra work, but it also increases the chances for scratching or nicking the vehicle's new paint.

There is no immediacy surrounding the detailing or reinstallation of dismantled parts, except the excitement of enjoying your entirely finished project, or the need to move on to other chores and projects. You should take your time to detail and assemble body parts carefully, so that they go on right the first time and look good once they are in place. This might be the last time you have the opportunity to clean and detail dismantled parts thoroughly. Since they are off the vehicle body, the jobs of cleaning, polishing, and waxing will not be hindered by their attachment to body panels or locations in confined spaces.

INSTALLING TRIM

Prior to reinstalling any pieces of removed trim, check to make sure that each one is not damaged and is clean and shiny. If the trim is metal, it will be easier to clean and polish if these tasks are done before the trim is re-installed. Plastic trim may be painted the same color as the body and, if so, should be checked for chips or other paint defects. If necessary, touch up any damage while the trim is still off the vehicle. With vinyl or rubber trim sections, you can treat them to a solid scrubbing with an all-purpose cleaner, such as Simple Green, and a soft brush. When they are dry, apply a satisfactory coat of vinyl dressing.

Rub the treatment in with a soft cloth or very soft brush. Be sure to wipe off all excess.

Make sure that all of the clips and retainers are on hand before attaching trim pieces. You will likely forget about any part that you installed with fewer than the original number of fasteners until it comes loose and breaks or causes problems. Secure each item properly before you walk away from it. Make sure you fully understand how they are intended to work before forcing them on inappropriately, and possibly breaking them in the process. As you did for their removal, have a helper assist you in replacing extra-long pieces. This will not only help prevent bends or wrinkles on the trim, but it will also add more control to the installation to circumvent accidental scratches on paint finishes.

Since door handles and key locks attach directly to painted body panels, you must install them with care to avoid causing scratches, chips, or nicks to the finish. In many cases, gaskets or seals are designed for placement between hardware and body skin. If the old gasket is worn, cracked, or otherwise damaged, do not use it because it will not perform its job properly. Wait until you have a new gasket to install that handle or exterior door item.

The screws, nuts, or bolts used to secure door handles are normally accessed through openings on the interior sides of doors. You have to reach through with your hand to tighten the fasteners. Be sure to use wrenches or sockets of the correct size to make this awkward job as easy as possible. After securing the handles and key locks, you must attach linkages or cables that run to the actual latch mechanisms.

As with the other exterior trim pieces and accessories, you should take this opportunity to clean, polish, and detail grille assemblies while they are off your car. Touch up paint nicks, clean tiny nooks and crannies, and wax metallic parts as necessary. Use a soft toothbrush and cotton swabs to reach into tight spaces. Should painted parts look old and worn, consider sanding and repainting them. Tiny chips or nicks can be touched up with the proper paint, using a fine artist's paintbrush.

A thorough cleaning with a soft toothbrush and mild cleaner should work well to remove accumulations of

Though obscured slightly by the raindrops, this hood trim chrome is in very good condition, although the paint is wearing thin on the bow tie. The painted area can be scuffed with some 400-grit sandpaper, cleaned with wax and grease remover, and then masked off and sprayed with the appropriate colors of touchup paint.

This air vent cover is easy to reinstall; it simply snaps into place. Most likely it would never be removed unless it was damaged in an accident, and then it would be replaced as this one has been.

polish, wax, and dirt from tiny corners and designed impressions, and make these items look like new. Be sure their fastening mechanisms are intact. Plastic emblems are not always easy to remove, and many times their plastic pins or supports are cracked during dismantling. If yours are damaged, you may have to replace them with new ones.

GRAPHICS OR ARTWORK

Most graphics are applied in a completely separate operation from the painting of the vehicle, long after the paint

guns have been cleaned and the masking paper taken off. The paint that you so carefully applied needs sufficient time to cure, so you don't trap solvents beneath the graphics.

Any time when painting graphics or any other artwork on your vehicle, using a basecoat/clear-coat system for the entire car will make for easier repair should you need to sand off overspray or other miscues. Most blemishes can be removed from the clear without affecting the color beneath it. However, if there is no clear to remove overspray from, you may easily sand through the color right into primer.

Left: *This cladding at the bottom of the door is commonly found on SUVs. It is typically secured in place with one or more rows of two-sided tape. There may or may not be alignment pins on this outer panel that would align with small alignment holes on the door.*

Below: *After verifying that the panel fits as desired, remove the protective cover from the tape on the back of the panel, align the pins (if present), and press the panel firmly into place.*

REASSEMBLY

REPLACING OEM ADHESIVE GRAPHICS

Although trim, emblems, and badges on contemporary vehicles are usually made of plastic rather than the polished chrome-plated metal of years ago, they still appear in some form on most vehicles. Plastic trim is usually adhesive backed, rather than being bolted on. Mike at Jerry's Auto Body makes installing a new piece of trim on the rear quarter of an SUV look pretty simple.

Left: By measuring the graphic on the other side of the vehicle, it was determined that the top of the emblem is $3/4$ inch below the bottom of the silver pinstripe. Since $3/4$-inch masking tape is very common, this emblem location is no surprise. As a guideline, a piece of $3/4$-inch masking tape is aligned at the bottom of the aforementioned pinstripe.

Right: To ensure that the emblem adheres properly, a bit of wax and grease remover is sprayed onto the application area, and then wiped off with a clean paper towel. This should remove anything that would prevent proper adhesion.

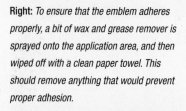

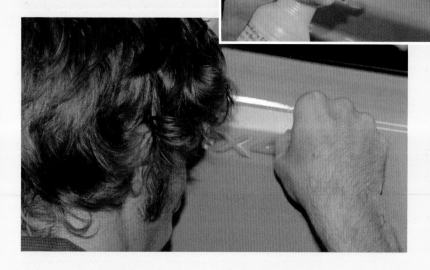

Left: The protective backing is removed from the adhesive on back of the "4x4" emblem. The top of the emblem is then aligned with the lower edge of the masking tape and pressed into place.

REASSEMBLY

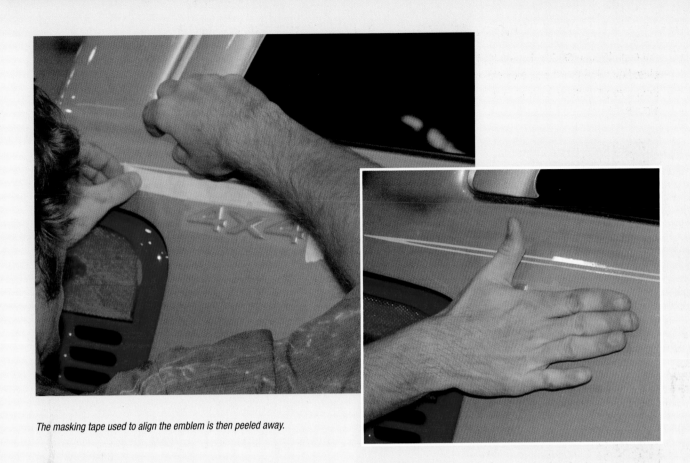

The masking tape used to align the emblem is then peeled away.

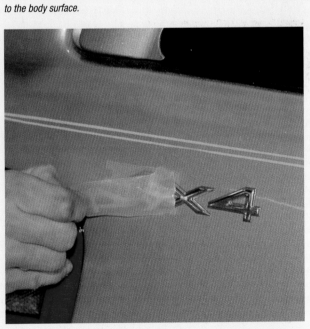

Firm and even pressure is then applied to the emblem to ensure that it adheres to the body surface.

The emblem's protective covering is then carefully removed.

After the protective cover is removed from the emblem, this portion of the vehicle looks just like it did when it was new.

Before adding any artwork, the entire area should be cleaned with wax and grease remover. Surface preparation will depend upon the media being applied, so read the instructions provided, or check with your paint and supply jobber.

Pinstriping

Pinstriping should be used as the finishing touch to any multicolor paint scheme, when chrome or stainless trim is not used, or it can also be a stand-alone accent to a single-color paint scheme. However a vehicle can begin to look too busy if pinstriping is used in conjunction with body side molding. Sometimes, less looks much better.

Common on factory paint jobs, pinstriping is usually a single or double line approximately $1/8$ inch wide and runs along the beltline or other bodyline of the vehicle, in a contrasting or complementary color. Since this application is as an accent, a bright color is common, such as an orange pinstripe on a maroon vehicle, or purple on a black vehicle. You most likely would not choose to apply a two-tone paint job using equal amounts of the colors just mentioned, but in the thin width of a pinstripe, it works well.

Graphics such as flames, scallops, or even lettering simply look more complete if outlined by tasteful pinstriping. Instead of two colors abutting each other, a pinstripe covers this otherwise unattractive seam of color. It can also serve to conceal slight irregularities in the edge of the paint that may have resulted from the removal of masking material. Whether necessary to hide miscues or not, no flame or scallop painting is considered complete if not pinstriped.

The most common paint for pinstriping or lettering is 1 Shot Sign Painter's enamel, which is available from larger art supply stores, some auto body paint suppliers, or through mail order from the Eastwood Company. It is relatively inexpensive and, with just a few primary colors and some extra mixing jars, you can use it to produce virtually any color. Before applying the pinstriping paint, use wax and grease remover with a clean cloth and then wipe the surface with a second dry cloth. You can apply painted pinstriping freehand by using a pinstriping brush (a dagger) or a mechanical device, such as a Beugler pinstriping tool.

Although it does take a little bit of practice, a Beugler pinstriping tool is much easier for the beginner to use to create consistent results. This tool is a small canister that is filled with paint and a built-in wheel that transfers the paint to the surface. The width of the wheel determines the width of the stripe, and heads with two wheels provide two stripes. The tool can be used freehand, but it will also accept a guide arm that can be run alongside a magnetic guide that can be aligned as desired on the vehicle's body.

LONG-TERM PAINT CARE

Contemporary catalyzed paint products are much more durable and robust than the lacquer and enamel products used in the past. Still, you cannot expect the paint on your newly repaired body to shine forever without some routine maintenance. Washing, waxing, and occasional polishing are essential if you intend to keep that new car appearance. By keeping a good coat of high-quality wax on your vehicle's painted exterior surfaces, you make them more resistant to dirt and road debris and also make washing your vehicle easier.

Unless this is a show-only vehicle that very seldom, if ever, gets driven, small nicks or chips will appear sooner or later. These blemishes will need to be repaired as soon as possible. If not, any exposed metal will begin to oxidize, which can spread under the paint and gradually undo your fine work. You have no doubt spent a significant amount of time and money repairing the damage to your vehicle, so you should maintain it to keep it looking good.

Washing, Polishing, and Waxing

Car wash soap products can be found at auto parts and discount department stores. For the most part, almost any brand of car wash soap should be well suited for the finish on your vehicle. Just be sure to read the label for any warnings and follow the mixing directions on labels of any product that you use.

The best way to prevent minute scratches or other blemishes on paint is to wash the vehicle in sections. Wash the dirtiest parts first, like the rocker panels, fender well lips, and lower front and rear end locations. Then, thoroughly rinse your soft cotton wash mitt and bucket. Mix up a new batch of wash soap to clean the vehicle sides. If their condition is relatively clean, you can continue with that bucket of sudsy water to wash the hood, roof, and trunk areas.

This process rids your wash mitt and bucket of dirt and other scratch hazards, like sand and road grit. If you were to wash your entire car with just one bucket of sudsy water, you would increase the chances of your wash mitt picking up debris from the bucket and rubbing that debris against the vehicle's lustrous finish. Likewise, any time when you notice that your wash mitt either is dirty or it falls to the ground, always rinse it off with clear water before dipping it into the wash bucket. This helps to keep the wash water clean and free of debris.

To clean inside tight spaces, like window molding edges and louvers, use a soft, natural hair, floppy paintbrush. Do not use synthetic-bristled paintbrushes because they could cause minute scratches on paint surfaces. In addition, wrap a thick layer of heavy duct tape over the metal band on paintbrushes. This will help to guard against paint scratches or nicks as you vigorously agitate the paintbrush in tight spaces and possibly knock it into painted body parts, such as those around headlights and grilles.

Many novice auto enthusiasts are confused over the difference between polish and wax products. Although both are paint finish maintenance materials, each has its own separate purpose. Polishes clean paint finishes and remove accumulations of oxidation and other contaminants. On the other hand, wax does no cleaning or shining. It does, however, protect those paint finishes that have already been cleaned and polished. Simply stated: polish cleans, wax protects.

Auto body paint and supply stores generally carry the largest selection of auto polishes and waxes, although many auto parts stores stock good assortments. Every polish should include a label that explains what kind of paint finish it is designed for—for example, heavily oxidized, mildly oxidized, and new finish glaze. Those designed for heavy oxidation problems contain much coarser grit than those for new car finishes.

Along with descriptions of the kinds of paint finish for which particular polishes are designed, labels will also note if the products are intended for use with a buffer. Those with heavy concentrations of coarse grit are not recommended for machine use. Their polishing strength, combined with the power of a buffer, could cause large-scale paint burning problems.

Carnauba wax is perhaps the best product to use for protecting automobile paint finishes. Meguiar's, Eagle One, and other cosmetic car-care product manufacturers offer auto enthusiasts an assortment of carnauba-based waxes. There are other paint protection products available that profess to work like wax, but they contain different chemical bases, which you must clearly understand before applying them to your new paint job.

Some of these products (typically, they have poly or polymer in the product name) are loaded with silicone materials. Although they may protect your car's finish for a long time, professional auto painters advise against their use, because the silicone content is so high and saturating that any future repainting that may be required could be plagued by severe fish-eye problems. In some cases, silicones have been known to penetrate paint finishes and eventually become embedded in sheet-metal panels.

If you find yourself in a quandary when it comes time to select a polish or wax product, seek advice from a knowledgeable auto body paint supplier. This person should be up to date on the latest product information from manufacturers and user satisfaction from professional painters and detailers in the field.

When to Wash New Paint Finishes

With newer paints with hardener additives, generally you can safely wash them after one or two days, as long as you use mild automotive soap products and practice gentle washing efforts. For uncatalyzed enamels, you should allot plenty of time (a few days or a week) for paint solvents to evaporate or chemically react before washing newly sprayed car bodies. To be on the safe side, verify with your paint supplier the required waiting time for the paint products you have purchased.

How Long Before Waxing?

Light coats of quality auto wax actually form protective seals on top of paint finishes. Even though they are quite thin and by no means permanent, these wax seals will prevent necessary solvent evaporation. Should that occur, those vapors that need to exit paint would be trapped. Consequently, as confined vapors continue their evaporation activity and persistence in reaching the open atmosphere, minute amounts of pressure are built up, which eventually cause damage in the form of blisters to the new paint finish. So, instead of protecting a paint surface, waxing too soon after new paint applications can actually cause unexpected damage.

You should wait at least 90 to 120 days before waxing your freshly painted vehicle. During the summer or in any location where the weather is warm and humidity is relatively low, 90 days should allow plenty of time for paint solvents to evaporate completely. When the weather is cooler or more humid, it takes longer for the solvent in the paint to evaporate, requiring a longer waiting time before applying wax.

While you are waiting to apply a good coat of high quality wax to the exterior, there are plenty of other things you can do to make your once crumpled or rusty car seem new again. Cleaning the windows inside and out, vacuuming the carpet, and cleaning the upholstery will make any vehicle more enjoyable to drive. Polish the chrome, scrub the tires, clean the engine compartment, and remove as much stuff as practical from the trunk. This once damaged vehicle is looking good again. I knew you could do it . . . .

SOURCES

Campbell Hausfeld
100 Production Drive, Harrison, OH 45030
www.chpower.com
888-247-6937, 513-367-4811
Air compressors and pneumatic tools

Car Quest of High Ridge
3032 High Ridge Boulevard, High Ridge, MO 63049
636-677-3811
Auto body repair supplies

Chief Automotive Systems
1924 East 4th Street, Grand Island, NE, 68801
www.chiefautomotive.com
877-644-1044
Chassis and unibody straightening equipment

Danchuk Manufacturing
3201 S. Standard Avenue, Santa Ana, CA 92705
www.danchuk.com
800-854-6911, 714-751-1957
Chevrolet restoration parts

Dupli-Color
101 Prospect Avenue NW500 Republic, Cleveland, OH 44115
www.duplicolor.com
216-515-7765
Paint products

Eastwood Company
263 Shoemaker Road, Pottstown, PA 19464
www.eastwoodco.com
800-544-5118
Specialty tools and equipment

Goodmark Industries
625-E Old Norcross Road, Lawrenceville, GA 30045
14820 Carmenita Road, Unit B, Norwalk, CA 90650
www.goodmarkindustries.com
770-339-8557 (Georgia)
562-282-0284 (California)
Sheet metal replacement panels

Hemmings Motor News
P.O. Box 100, Bennington, VT 05201
www.hemmings.com
800-227-4373
Classified ads for vehicles, products, and services

HTP America
3200 Nordic Road, Arlington Heights, IL 60005
www.usaweld.com
800-872-9353, 847-357-0700
Welders, plasma cutters, tools, and accessories

Jerry's Auto Body, Inc.
1399 Church Street, Union, MO 63084
636-583-4757
Auto body repair

Karg's Hot Rod Service
6505 Walnut Valley Road, High Ridge, MO 63049
www.kargshotrodservice.com
314-809-5840
636-677-3674 (shop phone)
Hot rod fabrication and repair

Mayhem Custom Paint and Airbrush
430 McArthur Avenue, Washington, MO 63090
636-390-8811
www.mayhemairbrush.com
Custom artwork

Meguiar's
17991 Mitchell South, Irvine, CA 92614
www.meguiars.com
800-854-8073, 949-752-8000
Car care products

Miller Electric Manufacturing Company
1635 W. Spencer Street, P.O. Box 1079, Appleton, WI 54912
www.millerwelds.com
800-4-A-MILLER, 920-734-9821
Welding power sources, plasma cutters, and welding accessories

Morfab Customs
301 South Pine Street, Union, MO 63084
www.morfabcustoms.com
636-584-8383
Hot rod fabrication and repair

Mothers Polish Company
5456 Industrial Drive, Huntington Beach, CA 92649
www.mothers.com
800-221-8257, 714-891-3364
Polishes, waxes, and cleaners

The Paint Store
2800 High Ridge Boulevard, High Ridge, MO 63049
636-677-1566
PPG paint products and supplies

PPG Refinish Group
19699 Progress Drive, Strongsville, OH 44149
www.ppgrefinish.com
440-572-2880
Paint products

Year One
P.O. Box 521, Braselton, GA, 30517
www.yearone.com
800-932-7663
Automotive restoration parts

INDEX

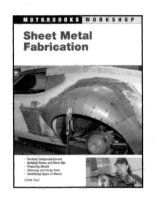
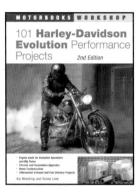

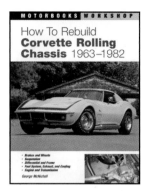
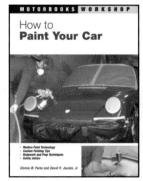